THE CORACLE

Raymond Rees, Secretary of The Towy Coracle Fishermen's Association,
at Carmarthen, 1987

The Coracle

J. Geraint Jenkins

Foreword by Raymond Rees

Golden Grove Editions

First published in part by David & Charles Limited,
South Devon House, Newton Abbot, Devon.

1988 © J. Geraint Jenkins

This edition published by The Golden Grove Book Company Limited,
Golden Grove House, 10 Quay Street,
Carmarthen, SA31 3JT, Dyfed, Wales in 1988

*Composed in 11/13 pt. Bembo type and printed and bound by
J D Lewis & Sons, Gomer Press, Llandysul, Dyfed, Wales*

Contents

List of Illustrations

Acknowledgements

For permission to use the photographs that illustrate the text we are indebted to the Welsh Folk Museum, St Fagans. The Frontispiece photograph is by Ken Towner by courtesy of Express Newspapers. The postcard material used to decorate the text is from the private collection of Thomas Lloyd and the new diagrams were drawn by Richard Jenkins.

Foreword

When I was invited to write a Foreword to this book, a revision of the coracle section of J. Geraint Jenkins's seminal work, *Nets and Coracles*, I had in mind the memory of the many pleasant hours I had spent recording for Geraint Jenkins, and thereby posterity, some of the information my grandfather, William Elias, had passed on to me during his ninety-eight year life time. Dr Jenkins and I have been friends for many years, and I was pleased to have the opportunity to put the record straight as far as coracle fishing is concerned, while at the same time being able to express my gratitude to him for his energy on behalf of the fishing industry in Wales. I hope this book, far more lucidly published in this new format, helps to bring about some closer understanding between the rod-and-line angler, the netsman and the general public.

Coracle fishing has always been surrounded by a mystique; deliberately of course, because in the days when it was the main source of income, food and survival, coraclemen only passed on their secrets to immediate family and never disclosed their catch, or where they caught it to anyone, especially to other coracle fishermen. It remains the case today, though it is hardly peculiar to river fishermen in Carmarthen.

The big difference now is that we no longer fish for a living, though it still is 'our way of life', something very difficult for the outsider to understand. Perhaps then, the reason why a craft and a skill recorded in the 11th century and earlier should have survived into the 20th century is that it represents a precious life-style in which the only discernible major changes are those of manufacturing materials. The shape and design of both the

xi

coracle and the net are peculiar to the river on which the craft is used. Formerly, coracles were used on most rivers, even in Scotland on the River Spey, and in Ireland on the River Boyne. In Wales, the Rivers Dee, Wye and Usk are well documented rivers where coracles were also used extensively. There is no doubt in my mind that if Julius Caesar had not seen a hide-covered boat resembling a coracle when he reconnoitred the south west coast of this country, thereby influencing his battle plans, history as we know it would have taken a different turn.

One of the biggest myths that surrounds the coracle is that our net stretches from one side of the river to the other and from surface to bottom. Nothing could be further from the truth. In fact, the Towy river coracle-net is only 40 feet wide and 36 inches deep. This dimension is further reduced overall by one third because of the arc of the trawling operation. Incidentally, coracle fishing is the oldest form of trawling and most of the commercial trawling operations have been copied from techniques practised by river fishermen.

Fish, especially salmon and large sea trout (sewin), can only be caught one at a time, because the net is too small and too fine to hold large fish for long, and there is no room in the coracle to handle safely two fish of 10lbs or more in weight. We do not sweep the river clean every time we make a trawl. This notion is not only absurd, but impossible. Our methods have stood the test of time; we have been brought up to crop the rivers with conservation uppermost in our minds. The river Towy and the rivers of Wales containing migratory fish would otherwise have been depleted of their salmon and sewin two-hundred years ago.

Without going into too much detail, the main skill required to be a successful coracle fisherman is to read accurately the state of the tides, the water's height and its speed and to be able to calculate how many pieces of lead of certain varying weights and sizes are needed to keep the net on the bed of the river, taking into account all relevant information, like wind speed and the state of the river before the tide. This includes such fundamentals as whether the river is in spate or not, which may sound complicated, but if you do not get it right you would be more likely to catch a fish in the public swimming pool!

These fine points represent some of the secrets handed on from father to son down through the centuries. With them came our own language, our own code of practice and our own code of laws, which are in addition to the laws and bye-laws governing net fishing as constituted and prescribed by the Water Authority.

Again to learn all the skills of the coracle-maker and the net-maker takes many years of diligent apprenticeship. The patient learning of what is not only a science but an art is extremely rewarding, and I suggest that is another reason for the ancient craft's survival. Perhaps too the uncertainty of the end result and the challenge of each new season. These have always held me in their fascination.

When monofilament nylon first came onto the market, it took me ten years to develop a net which could compete with the old linen and hemp nets. Eventually I was successful, and my design is in general use today. North Sea gas put an end to the local gasworks, so our readily-available cheap source of water-proofing material, pitch and tar, has gone the way of the wind. The local sawmills are now national companies with no facility for cutting home-grown and locally-felled timber, so it is very difficult to arrange for an ash tree you may have cut down yourself to be sawn into laths to make the framework for a wooden coracle. Add to this the construction of Llyn Brianne Dam at the headwaters, resulting in flow levels half those of sixteen years ago. Yet another change raises its head in the fibreglass coracle, a boat with anti-rot properties—but a rotten boat to ride in. Technology has even caught up with the coracle. But for me a wood and canvas boat and cow's tail ropes (that's another story) will never know a substitute.

Raymond Rees

Chapter 1

Introduction

The use of the coracle as a fishing craft on Welsh rivers has declined very rapidly in recent years, so that today coracle fishing is limited to three west Wales rivers—the Teifi, Towy and Tâf. Even on those rivers there has been a sharp decrease in coracle fishing. For example, on the Teifi, the picturesque village of Cenarth has long been regarded as the home of coracle fishing, but in 1972 no coracle fishermen at all operated from that village, the last licensee being unable to work after 1970. In 1807 there were so many coraclemen at Cenarth that a contemporary observer wrote:[1] 'There [is] scarcely a cottage in the neighbourhood without its coracle hanging by the door.'

The coracle, which is a keel-less, bowl-shaped fishing boat, has been known for many centuries in Wales and it may be regarded as the direct successor to the small skin-covered boats described in detail by Caesar,[2] Pliny[3] and other Roman writers[4]. It seems, however, that the vessels described by Roman writers as well as those mentioned in the *Mabinogion*[5] were sea-going, keeled boats, similar to the curraghs of Ireland,[6] rather than to the keel-less fishing coracles of Welsh rivers, that are specifically designed for operation in swiftly-flowing streams.

It is clear that in addition to the curragh type of skin-covered boat in use in the Dark and Middle Ages, fishing coracles were also in use. Little is known about their design, but in the *Gododdin* poem of Aneirin, which can be dated to the seventh century, one line reads *ef lledi bysc yng corwc*[7] (he would kill a fish in his coracle), while the medieval Welsh laws give the value of a coracle as eight pence *(corwc wyth keinhawc kyfreith)*.[8]

The first clear description of the true river coracle appears in the writings of Giraldus Cambrensis, who in 1188 made a journey through Wales. 'To fish or cross streams', he says,[9] 'they use boats made of willow, not oblong nor pointed at either end, but almost circular or rather in the form of a triangle, covered without but not within[10] with raw hides. When a salmon thrown into one of these boats strikes it fiercely with its tail, it often oversets it and endangers both vessel and boatman. In a clumsy manner, in going to or coming from a river, the fishermen carry these boats on their shoulders.' Unfortunately Giraldus gives no key as to where in Wales he encountered coracles. At Cenarth he provides considerable detail describing the salmon leap and the salmon fishing weir at Cilgerran and indeed he even describes the beavers that lived near the river at the time but he makes no mention of coracles at all. George Owen[11] in the early seventeenth century, gives many details of fishing weirs at Cilgerran and seine nets in the estuary but nowhere does he mention coracle fishing, though he describes the river at Cenarth in considerable detail. By the end of the eighteenth century coracles were very common indeed at Cenarth and a witness to the Royal Commission in 1863 strengthens the view that coracles were unknown on the Teifi until the latter part of the eighteenth century.[12] The witness said that coracles 'have increased since I have known Cenarth, which is the principal coracle station . . . Coracle fishing has not been introduced on the Teifi from what I can gather above 60 years or something of that sort'. The absence of evidence relating to the use of coracles for fishing in the rivers of south-west Wales before the second half of the eighteenth century is surprising. But in north Wales, especially on the Dee, coracle fishing was undoubtedly commonplace in earlier centuries.

Medieval *cywyddau* give some indication of the design of coracles in north-east Wales. In Cardiff MSS.64 and 12[13] they are mentioned. The first poem is by Ifan Fychan ab Ifan ab Adda soliciting a coracle from Sion Eutun. The second is a reply by Maredudd ap Rhys, who flourished between 1430 and 1450, on behalf of Sion Eutun. The third *cywydd* contains little relevant material on the design of coracles in north-east Wales.

Cywydd 1

Am gwrwgl i ymguriaw
Am y pysg drud cyn y Pasg draw
Crair lleder, croyw air Lladin
Codrwyn du, caeadrwym din
Cod groenddu da, ceidw grinddellt
Y gerwyn deg o groen du
Bwcled sad, ble cela" son
Bas ydyw o bais eidion
Padell ar ddwr ni'm pydra
O groen cu eidion du da

For a coracle to beat about
 For the valuable fish before next Easter
A leather relic, pure Latin word
Black covering enclosing its bottom
A bag of black skin, preserves dry laths
A fair vat of black skin
A firm buckler (why should I conceal it)
It is shallow, made of a bullock's tunic
A pan which will not cause me rot in water
Made from the fair skin of a good black bullock

Cywydd 2

Bola croen ar waith bual crwn
Bwlch byrflew tondew tindwn

Nofiwr o groen anifail
Noe serchog foliog o fail
Llestr rhwth fal crwth fola croen
Coflaid o ledryn cyflo
Myn Pedr, mae yn y lledryn
Rywiogaeth wyll a dwyll dyn
A elai'r cwrwgl dulwyd
I'r llyn a'r pysgotwr llwyd?
Er dim ni ddeuai o'r dwr
Heb ysgwyd i'w bysgodwr
O'ch Fair, pan na chai efo
Long o groen newydd flingo?
Groen buwch ar waith gweren bert

A skin bag in the shape of a circular horn
A short-haired, skinned box with broken bottom*
A swimmer of animal skin
A fond, paunchy vessel
An open vessel like a skin bellied *crwth*
An armful of leather in calf
By Peter, there is in the leather
The nature of a fiend that deceives man
Would the dark grey-black coracle
Take the fisherman to the pool?
Never would it come home from the water

---

* laths

4

Until it had given a push to its fisherman
By Mary! Why does he not
Have a ship of newly flayed skin
The skin of a cow worked with the fair tallow
      candle

One of the great advantages of the coracle over other types of fishing craft is its manoeuvrability and the fact that it only draws three or four inches of water. In shallow or rock-strewn rivers it is particularly useful not only for netting but also for angling. In eighteenth-century Monmouthshire, for example, the fishermen are said to have made use of 'a thing called Thorrocle or Truckle'[14] when fly-fishing for grayling. In the Dee, the coracle was regarded as essential 'on the rough, rocky middle reaches . . . when, owing to the force of the current and deep hidden ledges and clefts in the rocky bottom, wading is impossible in many places, and no other type of craft, not even a birch bark could possibly be used . . . A single coracle weighs some 30lb and a double one some 10lb heavier. In one of these it is possible to shoot rapids and dodge in between out-jutting ledges in the fastest and wildest stream, holding on by gaff or paddle to some outcropping ledge or rock, and one can turn oneself in perfect safety with a rush of wild white water on each side. By using a coracle one can therefore fish places that could never be reached either by wading or throwing the longest line from the bank'.[15] A practice not to be recommended!

Of course the coracle has always been used primarily for netting and both its manoeuvrability and lightness were important considerations in its persistence. The coracle fisherman usually had to carry the coracle on his back for considerable distances, for fishing is undertaken by drifting with the flow of river. 'It happened frequently', said a Report of 1861,[16] 'that several hundreds of men would go out very early in the morning with coracles on their backs, pass over the mountain and come some distance down the river, taking all they could catch with very fine nets.' Describing the lightness of the Monmouthshire coracles, Hawkins[17] says the coracle was so light that 'the countrymen will hang it on their heads like a hood, and so travel with a small paddle which serves for a stick till they come to a river, and then they launch it and step in; there is great difficulty in getting into one of those Truckles, for the instant you touch it with your foot it flies from you and when you are in, the least inclination of the body oversets it'.

When animal hides were used for covering the wooden framework of a coracle, the vessel was undoubtedly much heavier than more recent ones where flannel or canvas was used as a covering. 'Presumably it was when coracles were hide covered that the old Welsh adage took form which runs ''A man's load is his coracle'' (*Llwyth gŵr ei gwrwgl*). Today a coracle in south Wales seldom weighs as much as 30lb, surely a trivial load to carry. A hide-covered coracle would weigh nearly double this and would justify the proverb more fittingly.'[18] Until at least the early seventeenth century, the latticed wooden framework of a coracle was covered with horse or ox hide, the covering area of one hide governing the size of a one-man coracle. In some parts of Wales, particularly south-west Wales, flannel had replaced animal hides as a covering by the end of the eighteenth century and continued to be used until the mid-nineteenth century.

It has been suggested[19] that canvas was a cheap substitute for flannel, but even so according to Donovan 'flannel was of a more durable substance, [it] may be easier prepared and keeps out the water much longer than canvas'.[20] In the Llanegwad Vestry Book on 7 September 1798, the following entry appears: 'that John Harry, overseer, do purchase flannel and other things necessary to make a coracle for John Lot.'[21] During the first decade of the nineteenth century, however, skin-covered coracles were still to be seen, but they were rare[22] for 'a kind of coarse Welsh flannel . . . is generally made use of. The particular sort of flannel proper for the purpose, could be purchased a few years past at a low price, but it is at present worth two shillings a yard upon the spot where manufactured, and hence through notions of economy, canvass prepared in the same manner is becoming rather more universal than before'.

J. R. Phillips in 1867[23] says that flannel was used 'until recently' for covering coracles at Cilgerran, while a Cenarth coracle fisherman interviewed in 1961[24] said that his father used flannel for this purpose until about 1880.

This was obtained from the woollen mills of Dre-fach, Felindre, Carmarthenshire,[25] and it was prepared by dipping in a boiler containing a mixture of tar and rosin.

When a flannel was fully saturated, it was taken out of the boiler by four men, one at each corner, and laid down on the upturned coracle frame and tacked into place. This seems to have been the usual method of covering adopted throughout south-west Wales, but it is unlikely that flannel was used in other districts. Pennant, in his tour of North Wales,[26] remarks that coracles on the Dee 'have now lost the cause of their name, being no longer covered with *coria* or hides, but with strong pitched canvas', while Bingley, ten years before, remarks that Dyfi coracles too were covered with canvas rather than hide.[27]

On a print at the Carmarthen Museum, dating from 1794,

some indication of the design and covering of a Towy coracle appears in a verse that reads:

> Upon the glittering stream below,
> Those fishermen of courage bold,
> In numerous pairs, pursue their trade
> In coracles themselves have made;
> Form'd of slight twigs with flannel cas'd
> O'er which three coats of tar are plac'd
> And (as a porter bears his pack)
> Each mounts his vessel on his back.

Nevertheless, for at least the last eighty years, Welsh coracles have been canvas or calico covered, and flannel-coated vessels with three coats of tar have ceased to be used. The method of covering on the Teifi and Towy is to use unbleached, twill calico, 5 yards long and a yard wide, cut and then sewn up the middle. This is tacked to the coracle frame and 6lb of pitch mixed with half a pint of linseed oil is then boiled thoroughly, allowed to cool and then applied to the outside of the coracle. Preferably this is done in the open air on a warm day and a single coat of pitch is usually sufficient to make the coracle waterproof. In Cardiganshire and Carmarthenshire, covering or 'tailoring' coracles is usually considered as a woman's duty. But at Carmarthen, after tailoring, the woman is not allowed to touch the coracle.

The life of a coracle is finite. Many Teifi fishermen believed they should obtain a replacement every two years. Slight damage to the craft was repaired by applying a tarred patch over a tear or hole, but if repair was not possible, it was quite common for a fisherman to re-cover an old coracle frame with a new piece of pitched canvas or calico. To repair a hole or tear in the covering of a coracle a hot poker was applied to the pitch surrounding the tear until it had melted. A tarred calico patch was then applied over the tear and the hot poker used again to spread the pitch over the patch. If by any chance the coracle was holed while on the water, a piece of lard, which was always carried in the coracle, was stuck over the tear as a temporary repair.

The design of coracles and the methods of using them vary considerably from river to river. They differ according to the physical nature of the individual streams—whether a river be swiftly flowing or slow moving, whether it has rapids and much rough water and whether it is shallow or deep. Design varies too according to the preferences of the individual fisherman and whether a fisherman prefers a heavy or light coracle. A Teifi coracle, for example, can weigh as little as 25lb and as much as 36lb while length varies from 50 inches to 60 inches, the actual size and weight depending on the preference of the fisherman. Design varies too, according to the tradition of the various rivers, for in Wales a remarkable homogeneity in the design of coracles occurred on the various rivers, and distinct regional types were in existence for many centuries. For example, although the coracles of the Towy and the nearby Tâf are superficially similar in shape, the Tâf coracle, designed for use in a fairly narrow, swiftly flowing stream, is heavier than the Towy variety. Instead of the wattled gunwale of the latter, it has a planked gunwale. The Tâf coracle is sharper at the fore end and flatter at the other, and usually weighs about 33lb compared with a maximum weight of 28lb in Towy coracles. During one fishing season, in the late nineteen sixties, when a Tâf licensee was unable to make a coracle for his own use, a Towy coracle from Carmarthen was borrowed for the season. The Tâf fisherman was not happy with the design and performance of this vessel on the river and he soon reverted to the traditional coracle built by the craftsmen of Lower St Clears, specifically for the Tâf.

The Salmon and Freshwater Fisheries Act of 1923 put an end to coracle fishing on many rivers such as the Severn, and severely restricted the use of coracles on many others. Subsequent river authority bye-laws have caused an even more rapid decline in coracle fishing and in some districts the coracle is on the point of disappearing. For example at Cenarth on the River Teifi, long regarded as a centre of coracle fishing, legislation in 1935 prohibited the issue of new licences to fishermen in the non-tidal section of the river above Llechryd bridge. Consequently, the number of coracle licensees has declined so that today no coracle fishing at all is practised at Cenarth. It was estimated in 1861 that there were over 300 coracles on the river with about 28 pairs of fishermen above Llechryd Bridge.[28]

Below Llechryd Bridge however, where the river is classified as tidal, there was until 1987 no restriction but under a net limitation order imposed by the Water Authority the number is now limited to 12. The coracle men there use both the traditional, armoured coracle net and the now illegal set nets for catching salmon. Cilgerran gorge is an ideal place for using illegal equipment,[29] for it cannot be reached by road or footpath. A newspaper report, for example, notes that for the period June—October 1969, '81 illegal set nets laid by ''latter-day pirates'' were removed from Cilgerran gorge'.[30] The set net *(rhwyd fach)* is a single, unarmoured net 18 feet to 50 feet long, usually of fine mesh[31] attached to the river bank by means of a light stone, and the other end is spread out as far as it reaches into the river. Lead is fastened to the foot-rope and corks to the headrope. The net is usually placed in the water by a coracle man and it can only be used in fairly still water. 'Although corks are attached to the top of the net', says the 1971 *Report of the South West Wales River Authority*, 'there are sufficient weights on the bottom to sink the net below the surface.' In 1970 over 100 of these illegal nets were removed by water bailiffs dragging the river at nights.

Coracles are also found on the Towy, where twelve are licensed to fish for salmon in the river below the town. In the eighteen-sixties, according to the *Commissioners Report on the Salmon Fisheries*, no fewer than '400 men . . . supported themselves on the salmon and sewin fisheries'.[32] The report continues: 'To a poacher (a coracle) is invaluable . . . The coracle man is often lawless and always aggresive, he poaches private waters for years and claims a prescriptive right; he uses violence if he is very strong, he threatens if his opponent be not so much weaker than himself as to make violence unsafe . . . working without noise and at night and scarcely visible, they are difficult to detect, and if detected, almost impossible to capture, for a few strokes of the paddle will always place the river between the poacher and his pursuer'.

The authorities, even in the eighteen-sixties, were critical of the coracle as a fishing craft in non-tidal waters, for although 'in tidal waters they are a perfectly fair and legitimate engine . . . in the fresh and non-confined portions of the rivers, they are very destructive . . . if a fish shows himself in the day, his capture that night is nearly certain. Perfectly portable, the coracles are put in the river at the end of the pool, containing the fish, and it is swept again and again, if necessary until he is caught'.[33] The twelve pairs in use today between Carmarthen Bridge and the sea represent a considerable reduction in numbers since the nineteen-twenties, when in 1929, 25 pairs were licensed to fish from coracles. By 1935 the numbers had declined to 13 pairs 'under stringent regulations and subject to a licence fee of four guineas'.[34]

As on the Teifi an attempt was made to abolish coracle fishing on the Towy in the nineteen-thirties, but by 1938 'the Ministry appears now to be willing to tolerate netting as long as the number of coracles does not exceed in future, a dozen pairs'.[34] This was the position in 1971 when twelve coracle licences were still allowed.

On the Tâf, a short swift river that flows into Carmarthen Bay near the village of Laugharne, one licensee is still allowed to fish from a coracle. The fishermen based in the village of Lower St Clears are part-time workers and operate day and

Coracle Fishermen, Carmarthen

night during the months of March to August only. In the early nineteenth century, the Tâf fishermen were regarded as very efficient and one observer 'saw for the first time, those feats of dexterity which are required in the management of such a capricious vessel', despite the fact that he was familiar with other coraclemen 'of the Towy and other rivers'.[35]

The numbers of salmon and sewin caught by west Wales coraclemen in 1970, 1985 and 1986 are shown in Table 1 (*below*)

TABLE 1

River	Licensees	Licence Fee	Salmon Number	Salmon Weight lb	Sewin Number	Sewin Weight lb
1970						
Teifi	5	£15.37½	33	417	160	
Towy	12	£12.00	225	1789¾	992	2829½
Tâf	2	£12.00	39	329¼	104	238½
1985						
Teifi	14	£102.00	29		247	
Towy	11	£181.00	25		919	
Tâf	2	£ 95.00	26		191	
1986						
Teifi	11	£102.00	68		865	
Towy	11	£181.00	68		145	
Tâf	1	£ 95.00	4		93	

(Weights for 1985/86 not available.)

FOOTNOTES

1. Malkin, B H: *The Scenery, Antiquities and Biography of South Wales* (1870), Vol 2, p 206.

2. *De Bello Civile*, Book 1, Chap 4.

3. *Naturalis Historie*, Book 4, Chap 30 and Book 7, Chap 27.

4. For example, Caius Julius Solinus, Avierus and Sidonius Apollinaris all make references to skin-covered boats of the sea-going variety.

5. Evans, J Gwenogvryn (ed): *White Book of Mabinogion* (1907), p 47, 'par weithon wahard y llongeu ar ysgraffeu ar corygeu ual nat el neb y gymry'. The coracles were obviously designed for undertaking the long sea-voyage from Ireland to Wales.

6. Hornell, J: *British Coracles and Irish Curraghs* (1938), pp 74 et seq.

7. Williams, Ifor (ed): *Canu Aneirin* (1938), pp 44. Sir Ifor Williams suggests that the word 'coracle' is derived from the Latin 'corium'.

8. Williams, S J and Powell, J E: *Cyfreithiau Hywel Dda yn ol Llyfr Blegywryd* (1942).

9. Jones, T (ed): *Gerallt Gymro* (1938), p 203. This translation is more accurate than that of the 1806 ed of Giraldus de Barri, *The Itinerary of Archbishop Baldwin through Wales,* AD MCLSSSV III, P 332.

10. In the earlier translation the coracles of 'twigs . . . covered both within and without with raw hides' gives a false impression of their construction.

11. *Owen, George: Description of Penbrokshire* (1892 ed), pp. 118—119.

12. *Royal Commission to Inquire into Salmon Fisheries* (1863), p 141.

13. Cardiff Public Library. A translation of the *cywyddau* appears in Lord Mostyn and T A Glenn: *History of the Family of Mostyn of Mostyn* (1925), pp 35—41.

14. Hawkins, J: Izaak Walton's *Compleat Angler* (1760 ed), footnote, p 33.

15. Parry, J Hughes: *A Salmon Fisherman's Notebook* (2nd ed, 1955), pp 18—19.

16. *Report of the Commissioners appointed to Inquire into the Salmon Fisheries (England and Wales)* [1861], p 224.

17. Hawkins, *op, cit*, p 33.

18. Lloyd, J E (ed): *History of Carmarthenshire* (1939), Vol 2, pp 319—20.

19. Donovan, E: *Descriptive Excursions through South Wales and Monmouthshire* (1805), Vol 2, p 229.

20. Lloyd, *op, cit*, 2, p 320.

21. Donovan, *op, cit*, p 228.

22. Hornell, *op, cit*, p 16.

23. Phillips, J R: *History of Cilgerran* (London 1867), p 167.

24. F C Llewelyn, Cenarth.

25. Jenkins, J G: *The Welsh Woollen Industry* (Cardiff 1969), pp 247 —308.

26. Pennant, T: *Tours in Wales* (1810), 1, p 303.

27. Bingley, W: *A Tour Round North Wales* (1800), 1, p 470.

28. *Report of Commissioners, op, cit*, pp 140—2.

29. Infra.

30. *The Welshman*, 2 January 1970.

31. An example at the Welsh Folk Museum (Accession Number 69.113) measures 204 inches long, 32 inches deep, with a mesh of 2 inches from knot to knot.

32. *Report of the Commissioners, op, cit*, p 115.

33. Jones, J F: 'Salmon Fisheries 1863', in *The Carmarthenshire Antiquary*, 4 (1962—3), p 210.

34. *Ibid.*

35. Donovan, *op, cit*, 2, p 228.

Chapter 2

The Coracle Net

The coracle net used by west Wales fishermen at the present time is a movable drag net unlike any other net used in British rivers. The coracle nets used on the River Towy are especially complex, for the weights attached to the foot-rope of a net are evenly distributed to an intricate, pre-determined pattern, according to the state of the tide and the flow of water at any one time. Considerable knowledge and experience of local conditions are vitally important in the correct setting of the Towy net. Teifi nets on the other hand are much simpler and no rigid allowance is made for the amount of water in the river.

Basically, the coracle net is a shallow bag dragged along the bottom of the river, the mouth of which is kept open by towing it between two coracles. It consists of two sheets of hemp, linen or more recently bonded nylon, joined together at the top, bottom and sides. The armouring has a large mesh, the lint a much smaller mesh, and as the lint is much deeper being three times the depth of the armouring, it billows out as a shallow bag behind the armouring when the net is towed through the water.

The Teifi coracle net, according to Fishery Regulations,[37] consists of 'a single sheet of netting measuring not more than twenty feet in length and not more than three feet and nine inches in depth, and having meshes measuring not less than two inches from knot to knot or eight inches round the four sides and having attached round its four edges, and on one or both sides, a sheet of armour measuring not more than twenty feet in length and not more than two feet and six inches in depth and having meshes measuring not less than five and one-half inches from knot to knot or twenty-two inches round the four sides'.

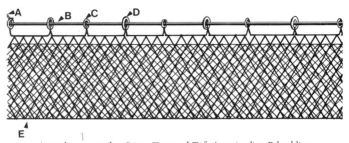

A coracle net as used on Rivers Towy and Tâf: A reeving line; B head line; C horn ring; D cork and horn ring; E foot rope

The Towy coracle net, on the other hand,[38] consists of 'a single sheet of netting measuring not more than 33 feet in lenth and no more than 3 feet 9 inches in depth, and having meshes measuring not less than one and a half inches from knot to knot or six inches round the four sides, and having attached round its four edges and on one side a sheet of armour, measuring not more than 33 feet in length and not more than 3 feet 9 inches in depth and having meshes measuring not less than five and one-half inches from knot to knot or twenty-two inches round the four sides'. There are many differences between the nets used by coracle fishermen on the two rivers, based not so much on legal requirements, but on tradition and on the customs of the fishermen. The Towy net is a far more sophisticated instrument than the Teifi and the complex and varied names for each part of the net suggests that the Towy net is possibly much earlier than the Teifi. On the Teifi, hemp has always been preferred for making nets, and although hemp is occasionally used on the Towy, the Carmarthen fishermen prefer linen thread, which they regard as being much stronger than hemp. In the eighteenth century flax was grown in the Towy valley and this provided the raw material for the net-makers of Carmarthen. There is no evidence to suggest that linen was ever used on the Teifi and the fact that the fishermen of Teifiside used imported hemp threads for their nets, again suggests a much later development. In recent years, bonded nylon has been used by Carmarthen coracle fishermen to make nets, although until recently the fishermen disliked synthetic fibre and clung to traditional materials for nets. On the Teifi, the head, reeving and foot ropes are always of horse hair, but on the Towy cow hair is used exclusively for the lines.

FOOTNOTES

36. I am grateful to Raymond Rees, Secretary of the Towy Coracle Fishermen's Association, for his assistance in the preparation of this section.

37. *South-West Wales River Board, Fishery Bye-Laws* (Llanelli 1970), p 6.

38. *Ibid.*

Chapter 3

The Teifi Coracle

The Teifi coracle, used by generations of fishermen at Cenarth, Aber-cuch, Llechryd and Cilgerran, varies little in shape and design from one part of the river to the other. According to Hornell,[41]'the Teifi coracle is characteristically short and of squat ungainly shape; in plan broad and with very little horizontal curve at the fore end; nearly semicircular in plan at the after end. At the insertion of the seat, placed about mid-length, the gunwale is pinched in at each side, giving the appearance of a slight waist between the forward and after sections. At the fore end and along the sides to a point just behind the seat, the coracle shows a slight degree of tumble-home, whereby the bottom view appears broader than the face plan and has no midships constriction, its outline being bluntly triangular, with all the angles well rounded. The apex, more rounded than the other angles, represents the stern. The gunwale sheers slightly towards the fore end, more emphatically towards the after end. The bottom is flat except for the last 12-15 inches, where it curves up gradually to the extremity of the stern. To anyone unfamiliar with these coracles, the narrowed and curved-up stern would seem to be the fore-end, whereas the wide and deep forward end would certainly be considered as the "stern".'

The framework of the coracle *(yr orage)* consists of seven longitudinal laths *(eisau,* sing *asen* or *eise hyd)* interwoven at right angles by seven transverse laths all spaced four or five inches apart. Crossing each other in front of the seat are a pair of diagonal laths *(eisau saethu,* sing *Asen saethu)* that are also interwoven with the longitudinal and transverse laths. As only one transverse lath is found behind the seat, this part of the coracle is strengthend by a semi-circular plait of hazel withies. Behind this plait the frame of the coracle is bent upwards to the stern of the vessel, and the position of the hazel plait marks the rear limit of the flat floor of the craft. To construct the coracle frame, willow branches are selected and cut; those for the longitudinal laths will be 7 feet 6 inches or 8 feet long and those for the transverse laths 5 feet or 6 feet long.[42] These are cut in the autumn or winter when they are not full of sap, the best quality willow being approximately seven-year-old pollard willow. In the past the demand for willow, which grows profusely in the Teifi valley, was considerable and willow trees were lopped at regular intervals. Today, however, with the disappearance of so many willow industries, harvesting is no

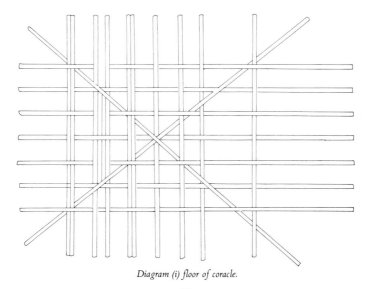

Diagram (i) floor of coracle.

19

Fred Llewellyn 'the coracle king' constructing a Teifi coracle.

longer a regular occurrence, and coracle builders are finding increasing difficulty in obtaining the correct raw material for framing coracles. With a billhook, each willow rod is split in half, so that the two sections are of equal thickness throughout their lengths. Each piece of timber is then placed in a shaving horse and smoothed with a two-handed draw-knife and spoke shave. The coracle builder's shaving horse is a low bench which the craftsman sits astride, pressing the clamping pedal with his foot, so that the lath, held fast by the clamp block, is held in the correct position for shaping. Before use, the laths are soaked in hot water or wrapped round with cloth dipped in boiling water so that they are more pliable. Seven laths are then laid on the floor, or on a wooden board, spaced 4 or 5 inches apart, and ten of the shorter laths are interlaced with them at right angles. The first group of transverse laths are laid close together in three pairs so as to provide added strength under the feet of the coracle man, so that, in reality, there are only seven transverse ribs in the coracle frame. The two long laths are arranged diagonally across the front of the laths and interlaced with the others. Heavy stone weights are placed at the intersection of the laths and the sides are bent upwards. A deal seat, about 36 inches long and 11 inches wide, is placed in position and the ends of the second and third transverse laths (counting from the back) are bent up and passed through slots made near the end of the deal plank. The ends of the two main longitudinal laths are next bent up and secured in the correct position by strings stretched between them. They serve as guides in the shaping of the hazel gunwale *(y blêth dop)* that is woven from a number of 9 foot lengths of hazel rods. The weaving usually starts from the left-hand side near the seat, and as the craftsman continues

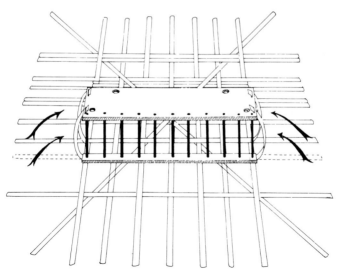

Diagram (ii) coracle seat in place.

William Elias constructing a Towy coracle

weaving towards the front of the coracle, the laths are inserted and carefully woven into the gunwale. The process is continued until the whole of the fore-part *(part bla'n)* of the coracle frame, which is almost a half-circle, is completed. At the back *(cwt y cwrwg)* one plait is bent down to form a strengthening band around the after end of the bottom, and a second is carried around continuously along the top, with the laths inserted into it. A third plait is then wattled on, although in recently made examples, a third plait is not used. When it is constructed, its withies are stronger than those in the other two, as this plait forms the margin of the gunwale and has to stand heavy usage.

John C. Thomas of Cenarth constructing a Teifi coracle.

23

It passes over the ends of the seat, which are thus sunk about 1½ inches below the top of the gunwale.[43] Nine or ten wooden stanchions, the lower ends sunk into a wooden bar turning transversely across the back of the coracle, are required to give strength to the seat.

The frame of the coracle is then complete, a coat of creosote is added as soon as it is dry, and approximately 4½ yards of unbleached calico, usually obtained from a Newcastle Emlyn draper, is stretched tightly over the frame and over the gunwale. The Teifi coracle differs from the Towy in that the gunwale is covered with calico without resort to nailing. The process of covering is known as *helingo* and the calico is sewn into place with twine or thin wire passed through the wattled gunwale. Finally a coat of pitch boiled together with linseed oil

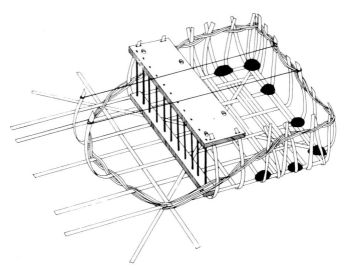

Diagram (iii) the plaiting.

Diagram (iv) helingo and pitching.

and possibly lard or tallow is applied hot to the outer surface of the coracle.[44] A dry day is usually chosen for this process of pitching the coracle *(pitsho cwrwg)*, sometimes carried out by women. Finally, a pair of holes is made at each end of the seat in order to fit the carrying strap of twisted willow, hazel or oak *(yr wden* or *gwden)*. The normal method of shaping the *wden* is to choose an oak sapling which is twisted, but to avoid cutting to within about 4 inches of the root. It is cut as near the root as possible. One end of the *wden* is passed down through the forward hole in a pair in the seat, and brought up through the after hole, thus locking it securely. The other end is treated similarly. Occasionally, a hole is bored just below the gunwale at the back of the coracle, so as to drain out the water when the vessel is carried ashore.

The paddle used on the Teifi is short and stouter than that used on the Towy. It is made of either larch, ash or elm and is 50 iches long. Most coracle men prefer larch paddles because they are lighter than those of ash or elm; an important consideration when they have to be paddled with one hand. The blade is 16 inches long, with sharp shoulders, and while one side is flat, the other is slightly rounded. The flattened top of the paddle ends in a claw which can be slipped under and thereby engage the basal bar of the seat support when the coracle is hoisted upon the owner's shoulders. The loom (that is the shank or handle of the paddle) 'rests on his right shoulder, and thus adjusted the pressure of the carrying rope across his chest is considerably reduced. The claw also affords a useful grip for the fingers of the right hand when paddling straight ahead with the paddle used over the bow; the left hand grips the loom about 15 inches lower down'.[45] The loom of the paddle is cylindrical in cross-section near its junction with the blade, but it flattens, and for the last 24 inches of its length it is nearly rectangular in cross-section to end in the claw. In paddling a Teifi coracle, a figure of eight motion is described in the water, and the paddle is kept continuously in the stream. When fishing, paddling is done with either the left or right hand, depending on whether the coracle is on the left or right-hand side of the river. The loom is gripped with one hand well below the middle and the claw of the paddle rests against the shoulder. When not netting, the coracle is propelled straight ahead by paddling over the fore end 'either by figure of eight stroke or by a scooping motion. In both cases, the paddle is gripped with the two hands, one gripping the claw at the top and the other holding the loom some distance down'.

Although all the Teifi coracles show remarkable uniformity of construction, the size and proportions can vary considerably according to the preferences of the individual fisherman. A tall and heavy man requires a larger coracle than a smaller man, who may require a lighter coracle for reasons of easy porterage. The following (*page 27*) are examples of the dimensions of Teifi coracles: Coracle A, now at the Welsh Folk Museum (Accession Number 04. 199) was made and used at Llechryd c 1890. Coracle B, also at the Welsh Folk Museum (Accession)

Number 51.252), was built by the Cenarth coracle builder, John Thomas, Bronteifi, in 1951. Coracle C, was measured by Hornell in the nineteen-thirties and belonged to Alfred E Griffiths, Cenarth.

	A	B	C
Overall length (along gunwale)	54 in	58 in	54 in
Maximum width (near fore-end)	41½in	39in	39in
Width (at seat)	34½in	34in	34in
Depth to underside of seat	12½in	12in	13in
Height from ground Front	18½in	18in	16in
Height from ground Back	19¾in	23in	18in
Width of seat	10in	9in	—
Weight	28lb	32lb	29lb

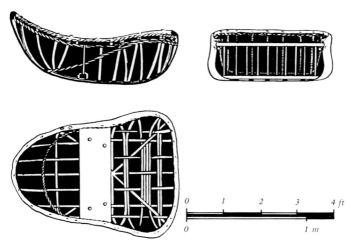

Diagram (v) The Teifi coracle.

27

In the nineteen-thirties a coracle would cost about £2 and there were two specialised coracle builders at Cenarth and another at Llechryd.

Coracles have been known on the Teifi from at least the last quarter of the eighteenth century, and many travellers to West Wales wrote of the coracles they saw at Cenarth, Cilgerran and Llechryd. H P Wyndham in 1781[46] for example, in addition to describing Towy coracles in detail, mentions them in use at Cilgerran, where they were used for ferrying people across the river in addition to fishing. 'The dexterity of the natives', he says, 'who fish in these coracles is amazing, though it frequently happens to the most expert, that a large fish will pull both the boat and the man under water.' Malkin, some twenty years later,[47] describes the Teifi coracle in considerable detail. 'They are made with very strong basket-work and covered with hides or coarse canvas, with a thick coating of pitch. Their shape resembles the section of a walnut shell, their length is generally five feet and their breadth seldom less than four. They contain but one person and it is entertaining to observe the mode in which they are managed. The dextrous navigator sits precisely in the middle, and it is no trifling part of his care to keep his just balance. The instrument with which he makes his way is a paddle. One end rests upon his shoulder, and the other is employed by the right hand in making a stroke alternately on each side. The left hand is employed in conducting the net, and he holds the line between his teeth . . . They are now applied only to the purpose of fishing.'

By 1861 the Teifi was regarded as 'the headquarters of coracle fishing', and the *Report of the Commissioners appointed to inquire into Salmon Fisheries* stated that fishing from coracles had been 'developed to the utmost . . . The feelings of the coracle fishers are strongly antagonistic both to the fishermen at the mouth' (i.e. the seine netsmen of the estuary) 'and to the upper proprietors. They form a numerous class, bound together by a strong *esprit de corps*, and from long and undisturbed enjoyment of their peculiar mode of fishing, have come to look upon the river almost as their own, and to regard with extreme jealousy any sign of interference with what they consider their rights. In the deep and narrow water near the Cilgerran slate quarries, several pairs of coracles are sometimes so arranged as almost entirely to close the passage against the fish'.

On the Teifi when coracle fishing was fairly unrestricted, as it was during the nineteenth century, the river was divided into four sections, the fishermen from one of four villages having the sole right to fish in those sections of the river. The four

Coracle fishermen on the Teifi, 1935.

Coracle men at Cenarth c. 1930.

villages concerned were Cilgerran, Llechryd, Aber-cuch and Cenarth. Each of these stretches of river was divided into a number of sections each being termed a *bwrw* (cast).[48] Each *bwrw* was divided into three parts, each of which was called a *traill* (trawl). At Cilgerran, for example, the principal trawl *(y draill)* was that side of the river usually, but not always, nearest the village; the second trawl *(yr ail draill)* signified the middle of the river and *yr hawel* or *tu'r dre* signified a third trawl, on the opposite side of the river from the principal trawl. 'If the principal trawl was on the Cardiganshire third of the river, the third trawl would occupy the third part of the river nearest to Cilgerran and was called *Tu'r dre* or next to the town, but if on the contrary, the principal trawl was along the Pembrokeshire third of the river, the third trawl would be . . . on the Cardiganshire side and would be called *yr Hawel*.'[49]

According to local tradition, each of the eight casts belonging to Cilgerran coracle men had its own characteristics, expressed in a doggerel verse passed down over many generations to the present day:

Bwrw byr hyfryd—Brocen ddryslyd
(Lovely Bwrw byr—complex Brocen)

Gwegrydd lana—Nantyffil lwma
(Cleanest Gwegrydd—Poorest Nantyffil)

Crow'n rhoddi—Pwll du'n pallu
([when]Crow gives—Pwlldu refuses)

Bwmbwll yn hela—Draill fach yn dala
(when one hunts at Bwmbwll—you may catch at Draill fach)

Each of the main casts had minor casts attached. Bwrw Byr had the minor casts of Pwll March and Gaing attached; Brocen had Bawbwll and Graigwen; Gwegrydd had Capel and Bwrw Oer; Nantyffil had Pwll Emlyn; Pwll du had Garw Bach and Garw Hir; Bwmbwll had Pwll-y-pysgod; Traill bach had Afr and Prior, while Bwrw Crow had no minor casts. In addition to the eight main casts and their subdivisions and accompanying minor casts, there were also eighteen other minor casts that did not belong to the principal ones. They were Pwll-y-Rhwyd (Netpool), Gaing, Pwll March, Bawbwll, Graigwen, Porthfa Lodge, Capel, Bwrw Oer, Pwll Emlyn, Pwll Elai, Garw Bach, Garw hir, Pwll-y-pysgod, Yr Afr, Y Prior, Traill y Bridill and Traill Silain (spawning shore) and Pwll Trewindsor.[50]

Travelling with a net on the Teifi at Cenarth.

'In or about the month of April', says the Cilgerran historian,[51] 'the town crier used to convene by a public cry, a meeting of all the fishermen for the season . . . ' Formerly none were permitted to fish in that part of the Teifi which borders on the confines of this parish, save those who had previously been admitted burgesses of the ancient borough of Cilgerran, so that the river being entirely monopolised by them, strangers were effectively excluded from participating in the fishery. At the annual April meeting of the fishermen the turns or casts for the first night of the fishing season were allocated. For this purpose, slips of paper on which were written the names of the eight principal *bwrws* and also of the subdivisions of each of such casts, were deposited in a hat, from which every fisherman in his turn picked out a slip and whatever name or position might be written on that slip would be his station during that first night. This arrangement, of course, only held good for the first

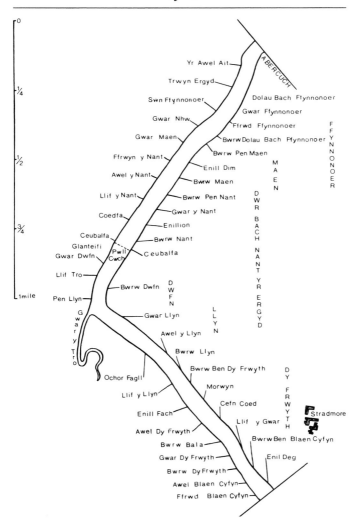

*The extent of the salmon fishing grounds of the Aber-cuch
and Cenarth coracle fishermen (continued on page 34)* ₹

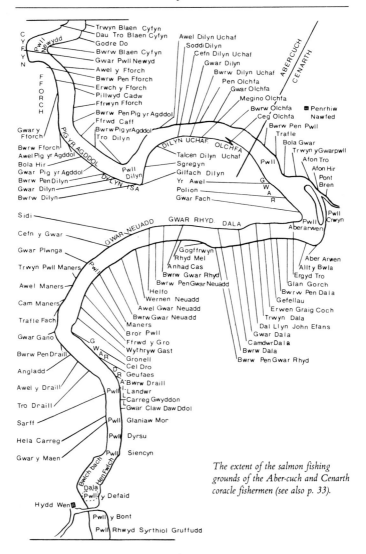

Trwyn Blaen Cyfyn
Dau Tro Blaen Cyfyn
Godre Do
Bwrw Blaen Cyfyn
Gwar Pwll Newyd
Awel y Fforch
Bwrw Pen Fforch
Erwch y Fforch
Pillwyd Cadw
Ffrwyn Fforch
Bwrw Pen Pig yr Agddol
Ffrwd Caff
Bwrw Pig yr Agddol
Tro Dilyn

CYFYN
PWLL Newydd
FFORCH
PIG YR AGDDOL

Gwar y Fforch
Bwrw Fforch
Awel Pig yr Agddol
Bola Hir
Gwar Pig yr Agddol
Bwrw Pen Dilyn
Gwar Dilyn
Bwrw Dilyn

Pwll Dilyn
DYLYN ISA

Awel Dilyn Uchaf
Soddi Dilyn
Cefn Dilyn Uchaf
Gwar Dilyn
Bwrw Dilyn Uchaf
Pen Olchfa
Gwar Olchfa
Megino Olchfa
Bwrw Olchfa
Ceg Olchfa

DILYN UCHAF   OLCHFA

ABERCUCH
CENARTH

Penrhiw
Nawfed
Bwrw Pen Pwll
Trafle
Bola Gwar
Trwyn y Gwarpwll
Afon Tro
Afon Hir
Pont Bren

Talcen Dilyn Uchaf
Sgregyn
Gilfach Dilyn
Yr Awel
Polion
Gwar Fach

Pwll
GWAR

Pwll Crwyn

Sidi
Cefn y Gwar

GWAR NEUADD   GWAR RHYD   DALA

Pwll Aberarwen

Gwar Plwnga
Trwyn Pwll Maners
Awel Maners
Cam Maners
Trafle Fach
Gwar Gano
Bwrw Pen Draill
Angladd
Awel y Draill
Tro Draill
Sarff
Hela Carreg
Gwar y Maen

PWLL

Gogffrwyn
Rhyd Mel
Anhad Cas
Bwrw Gwar Rhyd
Bwrw Pen Gwar Neuadd
Helfo
Wernen Neuadd
Awel Gwar Neuadd
Bwrw Gwar Neuadd
Maners
Bror Pwll
Ffrwd y Gro
Wythryw Gast
Gronell
Cel Dro
Geufaes
Bwrw Draill
Landwr
Carreg Gwyddon
Gwar Claw Daw Ddol
Glaniaw Mor
Dyrsu
Siencyn

GWAR
DRAILL
Pwll
Pwll
Pwll
Pwll

Bwlch bach   Hen Fwlch
Dala
Pwll y Defaid

Hydd Wen

Pwll y Bont
Pwll Rhwyd Syrthiol Gruffudd

Aber Arwen
Allt y Bwla
Ergyd Tro
Glan Gorch
Bwrw Pen Dala
Gefellau
Erwen Graig Coch
Trwyn Dala
Dal Llyn John Efans
Gwar Dala
Camdwr Dala
Bwrw Dala
Bwrw Pen Gwar Rhyd

The extent of the salmon fishing grounds of the Aber-cuch and Cenarth coracle fishermen (see also p. 33).

night, for he that would have the best chance on the first trawl on the upper cast on the first night, would be the last on the next cast on the following night, and so on until he had gone through all the subdivisions in each *bwrw*.' If a fisherman should absent himself from his station on any one night, no one could take his place, for the allocation of casts was very rigidly enforced at all times. The starting point of every station was termed *Pen bwrw* (the head of the cast), where the coracles were placed in order of precedence. 'The two leading coracles were required to be with their keels on the ground, in the same position as when on the water, with the paddle resting on the seat. If this rule was not adhered to, the owners of the leading coracles were deprived of their trawl.'

The rigid rules of precedence and privilege were undoubtedly framed by the fishermen themselves and were invaluable in that disputes were avoided. They were oral laws passed down from father to son and were practised with little variation by the coracle men of Llechryd, Aber-cuch and Cenarth as well as those of Cilgerran. Before the eighteen-sixties the close season for salmon fishing was largely a matter of unwritten law rather than of legislation and the season extended from August to February. One fisherman in each village was responsible for locking up the coracles during the close season.[52] In the eighteen-sixties, appreciable quantities of salmon were salted and smoked, and some fresh salmon was 'sent to London and those that are fit are sold to Londoners, and the rest are sent to France'.[53] In addition to coracle fishing at Cenarth, Llechryd, Aber-cuch and Cilgerran, coracle fishing was also practised up-river at Llandysul where coracle nets were in constant use for a few years. According to the Commissioners' report, coracle fishing had only been recently introduced above Cenarth Falls, and the evidence suggests that after 1863 when licences were introduced, coracle fishing at Llandysul disappeared.

In the coracle fishing villages below Cenarth Falls, fishermen flourished despite the introduction of a five shilling licence fee.[54] Nevertheless, the eighteen-sixties saw the end of the rigid rules of precedence that had been practised on the river. At Cilgerran, for example, the rules were disregarded ' . . . and recently the person who left the first coracle at a station during the day was entitled to precedence in trawling the following night, the river from that station to the next; but now before a person has any certainty of a draw, he must need place himself at the starting point and there remain with his coracle from the morning till the evening sets in, and the darkness enables him to spread his net to advantage; and even this patient watching does not always now secure a first position. In fact there is no regulation whatever adhered to; everybody scrambles for the first chance; and everybody spreads his net wherever he thinks it likely to obtain a fish'.[55]

Although the rigid rules of precedence had disappeared from Cilgerran by the eighteen-sixties, vestiges still remained until the nineteen-thirties. Cilgerran coracles that could fish between Llechryd and Cardigan Bridge fished well-defined pools - Y Gwddwg, Llyn, Pwll byr, Y Frocen, Gwaun Morgan, Y Cafan, Nantyffil, Y Crown, Bwmbwll, Bwrrwyd, March, Pen Pwll, Pysgod, Chwarel Aubrey, Y Gwter, Yr Afar, Y Prior, Ben Jubilee. The first pair of coracles at a particular pool could enter the water first. This first pair were known as *yr ergyd*. It was then followed by *yr ail draill* that could enter the water as soon as *yr ergyd* had drifted 50 yards from the start of the trawl. This was then followed by *y trydydd* (the third); but the first pair could not begin a second trawl until the third had completed its first.

It may be suggested that one of the factors that contributed to the relative decline of the old system of pool allocation in the sixties and seventies was the arrival of the railway, which brought the Billingsgate fish market within very easy reach. An increasing number of fishermen owned a net and the coracle men forgot time-hallowed codes and fished where they would. The railway that came to Carmarthen in 1852, Whitland in 1854 and Cardigan in 1880, extended the fisherman's market and gave a powerful incentive to the netsmen of the Teifi to increase their activity and catches of salmon now that they would be transported with much greater ease to a mass market. Consequently, the local Teifi-side custom of salting and smoking salmon for preservation declined greatly.

Today the licence fee for a coracle net is £181.00 and there has been a rapid decline in the use of the coracle as a fishing craft on the river. In 1861, a witness thought that there were well over 300 coracles on the river. Another witness thought that there were between 200 and 300 coracles at Cilgerran alone, and that 'almost everybody in Cilgerran has a coracle'. At Cenarth, however, there were only 16 or 18 nets, while Abercuch had 10. The close season, by general agreement of the fishermen themselves, extended from 3 November to 3 March. Even in 1861 coracle fishermen had aroused the wrath of the rod and line anglers, for 'these coracles fish down the stream . . . and render the river unfit for rod or fly fishing'.[56]

After the eighteen-sixties, with the enactment of a number of Acts designed to limit and control salmon fishing,[57] close seasons and licensing of coracle fishermen were introduced. The close season varied, but it usually extended from 31 August to

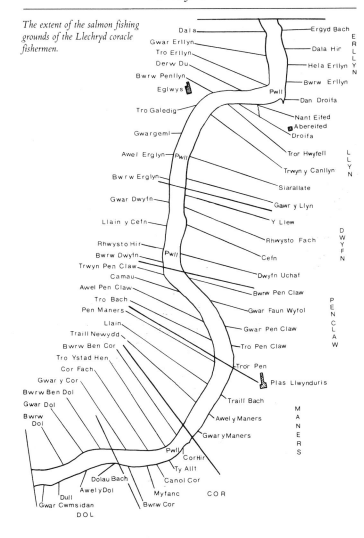

The extent of the salmon fishing grounds of the Llechryd coracle fishermen.

Dala
Gwar Erllyn
Tro Erllyn
Derw Du
Bwrw Penllyn
Eglwys
Tro Galedig
Gwargeml
Awel Erglyn — Pwll
Bwrw Erglyn
Gwar Dwyfn
Llain y Cefn
Rhwysto Hir
Bwrw Dwyfn — Pwll
Trwyn Pen Claw
Camau
Awel Pen Claw
Tro Bach
Pen Maners
Llain
Traill Newydd
Bwrw Ben Cor
Tro Ystad Hen
Cor Fach
Gwar y Cor
Bwrw Ben Dol
Gwar Dol
Bwrw Dol
Dolau Bach
Awel y Dol
Dull
Gwar Cwmsidan
DOL

Pwll

Ergyd Bach
Dala Hir
Hela Erllyn
Bwrw Erllyn
Dan Droifa
Nant Eifed
Abereifed
Droifa
Tror Hwyfell
Trwyn y Canllyn
Siarallate
Gawr y Llyn
Y Llew
Rhwysto Fach
Cefn
Dwyfn Uchaf
Bwrw Pen Claw
Gwar Faun Wyfol
Gwar Pen Claw
Tro Pen Claw
Tror Pen
Plas Llwynduris
Traill Bach
Awel y Maners
Gwar y Maners
Pwll
Cor Hir
Ty Allt
Canol Cor
Myfanc
Bwrw Cor
COR

ERLLYN
LLYN
DWYFN
PEN CLAW
MANERS

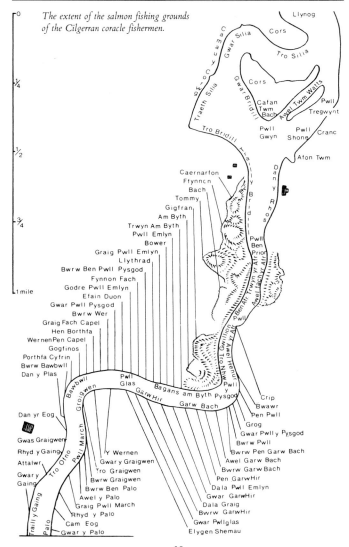

The extent of the salmon fishing grounds
of the Cilgerran coracle fishermen.

39

1 February with a close time at weekends. Nevertheless, coracle fishing flourished throughout the last quarter of the nineteenth century and the first thirty years of the present century, with the result that in 1932 there were 24 coracle net licences, involving the use of 48 coracles at Cenarth alone, with a further estimated 52 netting permits below Llechryd Bridge.[58] By 1935, 33 netting licences had been issued.[59] The enactment of a bye-law, confirmed by the Ministry of Agriculture and Fisheries on 14 February 1935,[60] put severe restrictions on coracle fishing in the non-tidal section of the river. Today coracle nets may only be used by a person who immediately before the coming into operation of this bye-law was permitted to use a coracle net in the water above the bridge.[61] As a result of the 1935 bye-law, coracle fishing has virtually disappeared in the non-tidal section of the river. In 1952 16 coracle licences were issued for fishermen between Llechryd and Cenarth; in 1957 the number of licences had declined to 4, in 1970 to 1 and in 1971 no licences at all were issued because the licence died with the licensee in non-tidal water.

The 1935 bye-law meant that coracle licences were not transferable as they are in the tidal reaches of the river, where at Cilgerran 5 licensees are allowed to fish from coracles. It has always been customary on the Teifi, which has always (until 1987) been an unrestricted river, for each licensee to be able to endorse two other names on his licence. Each endorsee (known locally as *gwas*) was expected to pay a shilling to the licensee for endorsement, and each one could operate the coracle without the licensee, as long as the licensee did not require the coracle himself. As a result of the 1987 legislation the licensee must now always be present. At Cilgerran, early in the twentieth century it was customary for an endorsee to apply for a licence

Boy in a coracle, from the Stackpole album.

of his own after three seasons as a servant. Undoubtedly, it is the rights of the rod and line fishermen that contributed indirectly to the disappearance of the coracle from the non-tidal reaches of the Teifi. As a report on salmon fisheries said,[62] 'There is no doubt that interest in angling has vastly increased of recent years and that the increase is continuing; anglers contribute greatly to the tourist industry and to the fishing tackle trade; some pay rates on sporting property to the local authorities in whose areas their waters lie and most contribute substantially to the funds of river boards through licence duties. On the other hand commercial fishing employs comparatively few people and none of them is employed in the business all the time for there is a close season of at least five months; most of the fishing is done in public waters and there is therefore no contribution to local rates; and the amount of licence duty paid by netsmen is only in a few areas a noticeable contribution to the income of the river board.'

41

Today the coracle fishing season extends from 1 March to 31 August; night fishing was not allowed in non-tidal reaches by the law of 1912, and the river is closed from 6am on Saturday to midday on the following Monday. Now no fishing is allowed by law in non-tidal reaches. The net is limited to a length of 20 feet and a depth of 3 feet 9 inches with a 2 inch mesh for the lint and 5½ inches for the armouring. Both coracle and net have to carry a licence number.

The salmon catches are today sold locally, but during the first quarter of the present century, Cilgerran had two fish merchants and Cardigan one, who paid regular visits to the river bank to purchase the salmon catches. In the nineteen hundreds, for example, merchants used to visit the river banks daily, paying about 2s 6d or 3s 0d a pound for the salmon.

Today all coracle fishermen are part-timers but until 1939 coracle fishermen working full days on the river were commonplace. During the closed season, many used to migrate to the coal mines of South Wales or were employed locally as quarrymen or rabbit catchers.

Coracles used on the River Nevern in north Pembrokeshire were similar to those of the Teifi, but even in the heyday of coracle fishing in the eighteen-sixties no more than four coracles, based at Newport, operated above the tideway. They and the seine netsmen of the estuary were at constant loggerheads for 'the men that fish the sand and those who fish the river are quite different men; the coracles belong to the men who fish the river and they are the men who give the most trouble; the men at the mouth of the river are fair fishermen'.[63]

The Teifi Coracle Net

The Teifi coracle net is 20 feet long and no more than 3 feet 9 inches deep. The mesh of the armouring can vary from the top to the bottom of the net, with the result that the top row of meshes, stapled by the third to the head-rope, may be no more than a couple of inches wide, while the remaining meshes may be of the full legal dimensions. In use, the top row of meshes will be stretched out to be almost parallel to the head-rope, so that in effect the armouring presents a wall of fine meshes when the net is drawn through the water. At Llechryd, the bottom row of meshes and the armouring *(y fras* or *y cefen)* is considerably larger than at Cilgerran or Cenarth, because of the rocky nature of the river bottom in that particular stretch of river. About 1½lb of hemp is required to make a coracle net, but the mesh of those nets may vary according to the time of year when it is used. In March and April when a run of large salmon is expected, a lint mesh of 6 inches is used, while in May and June, to catch small salmon *(Meillion Mai)* a smaller mesh is required.

The foot-rope *(blwm-ffun)* is made of a three-ply *(teircain)* plait of horsehair which does not absorb water and this is leaded at regular intervals with lead weights. Pieces of lead cut from sheet lead into rectangles of 2 inches by ¾ inches are pressed into shape on the foot-rope. When the river is in flood it is necessary to add more weights to the net to ensure that it sinks properly in the water. The net is suspended from a head-rope *(ffenest-ffun)* which is again made of three-ply horsehair, which according to one Cilgerran fisherman 'should be thinner than my little finger'. This is connected to the net at intervals of three or four meshes. In Teifi nets, no corks are attached to the coracle net. The stapling line *(traill-ffun)* is attached to eleven or more horn rings, threaded and running on the end rope. To make these rings, a cow horn is boiled until soft and moulded on a piece of wood. The horn is then sawn into ¼ inch rings. At one end the stapling line is made fast to a non-running horn ring lashed on to the head-rope; the outer end is tied to the last of the running rings at the opposite end of the net. To the same ring is attached one end of a long reeving line *(ffun fowr)* of which the other end is free. The reeving line is considerably thicker than the other lines in the net, 'three times as thick as the small finger' and is usually plaited from six hanks of horse hair. The horn rings are attached to the head-rope at approximate intervals of 22½ inches. The net itself is about 90 meshes wide and on the Teifi it is measured by the *gwrhyd* (ie *gwr* [man] and *hyd* [length]—the distance measured by the fully outstretched arms of a man). The reeving line between the edge of the net and a coracle should be two *gwrhyd* long.

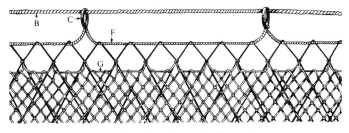

Detail of top of a Teifi coracle net: B headline; C horn ring;
F stapling line; G marrying.

In use, the net is carried to the river bank on top of the coracle carried over the shoulders of the fisherman allocated to the right-hand side of the pair of coracles. It is the senior partner who always takes the left-hand bank, and it is his invariable duty to draw in the net when fishing. On reaching the river bank, the net is carefully arranged and the pair of coracles enter the river drifting into the flow in mid-stream. 'The coracles will be about four or five yards apart', says one fisherman.[39] The net will be between them, the left-hand fisherman holding both reeving line and head-rope, the right-hand fisherman holding the reeving line only. When a salmon strikes the net, the right-hand man *(dyn llaw dde)* throws the reeving line and the net closes as his partner pulls it in to his side of the river. As the left-hand man *(dyn llaw whith)* draws in the net, the right-hand coracle comes up behind him, grasping the gunwale of the other coracle to prevent it drifting with the flow of the water *(colli dwr*, ie 'losing water'). Contrary to general belief, a salmon is never seen 'jumping in the river'; if one is seen, it is certainly a kelt and not worth catching. The action of a coracle net, therefore, is that where the reeving line is thrown by one fisherman, the strings attached to the horn rings shut together along the head-line, thus bunching the armouring meshes together. In turn, the lint meshes bunch together, so that the salmon is caught in a bag formed by the lint and armouring. At the end of a trawl, the pair of fishermen land on the river bank; they heave the coracles on their shoulders and the senior partner arranges the net and throws it on top of his mate's coracle. They then walk back to the beginning of the trawl again.

FOOTNOTES

39. J M Griffiths, Cilgerran, Pembrokeshire. Welsh Folk Museum Record 3309.

41. Hornell, *op, cit*, p 23.

42. I am grateful to the late Mr John Thomas, Bronteifi, Cenarth for a great deal of information on coracle building methods.

43. Hornell, *op, cit*, p 24.

44. The usual quantity required is 6lb pitch, ½lb linseed oil or with ½lb or less of lard. Oil and lard are added in order to prevent the pitch from becoming brittle and peeling off.

45. Hornell, *op, cit*, p 26.

46. Wyndham, H P: *A Tour through Monmouthshire and Wales . . . 1774 . . . and 1777* [1781], p 86.

47. Malkin, *op, cit*, 2, pp 206—7.

48. The principal casts of Cilgerran fishermen who operated between Tro'r Llyn to within half a mile of Cardigan bridge were—Bwrw byr, Brocen, Gwegrydd, Nantyffil, Crow, Pwlldu, Bwmbwll, Traill Bach. Between Tro'r Llyn and Cwm Sidan, Llechryd coracle men were responsible for fishing. Their principal casts were Bwrw Llyn, Gwddwg, Llyn Ffranc, Pwllglas, Pwlldu, Erllyn, Penllyn, Erglyn, Dwyfn, Penclaw, Maners, Cor and Dôr

Between Cwm Sidan and Allt Stradmore, Aber-cuch fishermen fished Ffynnonoer, Maen, Dŵr Bach, Nant-yr-ergyd, Dwfn, Dyfrwyth, Blaen Cyfyn, Pwll Newydd, Fforch, Pig-yr-Agddoe, Dilyn isa, Pwll Dilyn, Dilyn Ucha, and Olchfa.

The Cenarth coracle men operated in Pwll, Gwar, Aberarwen, Dala, Gwar rhyd, Gwar Neudd, Gwar draill, Hen fwlch and Bwlch Bach..

49. Phillips, J P: *History of Cilgerran* (1867), p 176.

50. *Ibid*, p 176.

51. *Ibid*.

52. Oral evidence F C Llewelyn. Welsh Folk Museum Record No 111A4.

53. *Minutes of Evidence taken before the Commissioners Appointed to inquire into Salmon Fisheries (England and Wales)* (1861), p 147.

54. A number of Cenarth fishermen refused to pay the licence fee and some were imprisoned for a month.

55. Phillips, *op, cit*, p 178.

56. *Minutes of Evidence, op, cit*, p 141 *et seq*.

57. Salmon Fishery Acts 24 and 25 Vict. c 109 (1861), 26 and 27 Vict. c 10 (1863), and 28 and 29 Vict. c 121 (1865).

58. *Tivy Side Advertiser*, 10 July 1932.

59. Hornell, *op, cit*, p 13.

60. Bye-Law 6E (Teify and Ayron Fishery Board) 'Prohibitions applicable to particular parts of the Fishery District'.

61. *South-West Wales River Authority Bye-Laws* (1967 ed), p 9.

62. *Report of Committee on Salmon and Freshwater Fisheries* (1964), p 13.

63. *Minutes of Evidence, op, cit*, (1861), p 136.

Chapter 4

The Towy Coracle

On the River Towy in the tidal reaches below Carmarthen town, twelve pairs of coracles are licensed to fish.[64] Most of the fishing is done at night between the old railway station at Carmarthen and the mouth of the river three miles upstream from Ferryside.[65]

There has been an equal decline in coracle fishing on the Towy and on the Teifi. Although in the early nineteen-twenties there was no limitation on the number of coracles operating on the river, the total number of coracles in use did not exceed 48 pairs. By the end of the decade, however, the number of licences had declined to 25[66] and by 1939 only 12 licences were issued. Since that date the number has remained constant, for fishery regulations state that new licences may be issued as long as the total number of licences does not exceed 12. Each licensee can endorse up to three other men on his licence, but he has personally to be present during a fishing session. Nevertheless, compared with the total number of fishermen operating in the nineteenth century, the decline since 1918 has been substantial. According to one witness to the Royal Commission in 1861[67] so many salmon were caught by coracle fishermen that they were 'salted and sold as dried fish in the town and country and sent away. They used to be hawked about the streets' (of Carmarthen) 'by the fishermen's wives and by the fishermen and in the country along the side of the Towy'. Another witness to the Commission noted that the Towy was being fished to such an extent that there was a scarcity of salmon in the Carmarthen district. This he attributed to 'the opening of the railways . . . Those who catch

47

the fish now have a certain instead of uncertain market . . . Our local supply had been more affected by railways than any other cause'. It was estimated that in the eighteen-sixties there were about 'two hundred coracle men on the river who had no other employment but salmon and sewin fishing'.

The history of coracle fishing on the Towy as on the other rivers of west Wales is obscure, but by the turn of the eighteenth century they were so common in Carmarthen 'that they cannot easily escape the attention of the tourist'.[68] Wyndham in 1781[69] describes how 'The fishermen in this part of Carmarthenshire use a singular sort of boat called coracles. They are generally 5½ feet long and 4 broad, their bottom is a little rounded and their shape nearly oval. These boats are ribbed with light laths or split twigs, in the manner of basket work, and are covered with raw hide or strong canvas, pitched in such a mode as to prevent them leaking. A seat crosses just above the centre, towards the broader end. They seldom weigh more than between 20 or 30 pounds. The men paddle them with one hand while they fish with the other'. John Evans on his visit to the Towy[70] describes the coracle fishermen as 'the Caermarthen victuallers . . . on account of the quantities of salmon they supplied to the town'. According to the *Second Annual Report of the Inspectors of Salmon Fisheries*[71] 'within the bay and tidal portions of the river no less than 400 men have for some years supported themselves and their families, two thirds of the year, on the produce of the salmon and sewin fisheries'. These included '12 to 15 long nets' as well as coracle nets. 'The coracles work in pairs', the Report continues, 'two of these hide boats with a man in each and a net stretched between them, drop down with the current. When a fish strikes they paddle rapidly together, and the fish and net are instantly landed in one coracle or the other'. The Towy coracle man was described in the Report as being 'lawless and often aggressive, he poaches private waters for years and claims a prescriptive right; he uses violence if he be very strong, he threatens if his opponent be not so much weaker than himself as to make violence safe. A man of some property in this part of the country told me that they had encroached upon his water and taken possession of it; that he did not dare to interfere, for they would burn his stacks. This year, on the Towey, they went in a body to Ferryside, where the long-net men mostly live, attacked the men and destroyed their nets . . . The evil is at present grave'. Earlier, according to the *Reports on Education in Wales* of 1847,[72] some 1,500 people living in Carmarthen derived their living from the fisheries on the Towy, 'and as their work was seasonal, they were frequently destitute on that account as well as because of their improvidence.[73]

The Towy coracle is longer and more elegant than the short, squat Teifi type. The following are examples of the dimensions of three typical examples: Coracle A now at the Welsh Folk Museum (Accession Number 32-250/1) dates from the nineteen-twenties. Coracle B and Coracle C were measured by Hornell.[74]

	A	B	C
Overall length	67in	68½in	64in
Maximum width (near far end)	43¾in	40½in	40in
Width (at seat)	40in	39in	39in
Depth (amidships to gunwale)	15¼in	15½in	16½in
Height from ground Front	15½in	16in	18in
Height from ground Back	13in	18½in	20in
Width of seat	10½in	10¾in	11in
Weight	32lb	31½lb	28lb

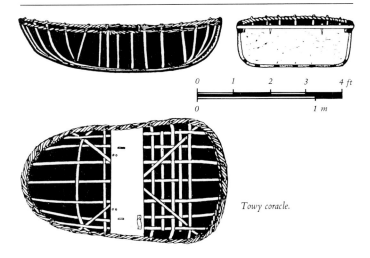

Towy coracle.

Towy coracles differ in construction from the Teifi in the following respects:

1. Sawn or split ash or willow laths rather than cleft willow rods are used for the framework of the coracle. As on the Teifi seven longitudinal and seven transverse laths are used, but on the Towy coracle 'the fore compartment is strengthened, not by doubling the three transverse frames, but by interlacing four short lengths *(ise dan drâd)* of lath alternately with the first four transverse frames. The accessory laths do not extend up the sides'.[75]

2. A leather carrying strap *(strapen gwddwg)* replaces the twisted withy, hazel or oak *gwden* of the Teifi coracle.

3. There is no plaited band to reinforce the after end of the bottom framing as on the Teifi coracle.

4. Although in recently made Towy coracles waterproof cloth coverings and a gunwale built up of sawn laths have

replaced plaited hazel or willow, in older examples a visible plaited gunwale is an outstanding feature of the Towy coracle. Although this gunwale is no deeper than that of the Teifi coracle, it has the appearance of being so, in that it is not covered with pitched canvas. On the Teifi coracle the calico is bound over the top of the gunwale with wire, but on the Towy vessel it is turned back and tied with string to the lath frames below the top of the gunwale. This is because the Teifi coracle-maker uses no nails in construction.

5. The Towy coracle is equipped with a half round band of ash *(gwragen)* on the outside at the bow of the vessel to give protection to the front, where wear and damage is most likely to occur.

6. The after region of the seat is supported upon a solid wooden bulkhead *(astell orles)* held in place by three long pegs driven through the seat. The bulkhead is used for carrying the net or a salmon and differs considerably from the vertical railed seat support of the Teifi coracle. The bottom of the bulkhead is wired or tied to the laths.

To make a Towy coracle, ash laths are preferred to withy laths, and from an ash pole 6 inches in diameter it is possible to obtain 30 laths. The ash is felled in the winter months and after splitting with a billhook or sawing in the local saw mills, the laths are placed in running water for two or three days, to facilitate bending. The seven longitudinal laths, the seven transverse laths and the two diagonal laths, each 1⅛ inches to 1¼ inches wide, are interlaced in position on a flat plot of ground. Wooden boards and flooring are never used by Towy coracle builders. 'Instead of fixing their position by superimposed weights' (as on the Teifi) 'the main crossings, those near where the laths are to be bent up are kept immovable

A Towy coracle.

by means of forked pegs, called hooks, driven into the ground
in such a way that the forked ends straddle the crossings of the
laths at all important points. From ten to sixteen of these hooks
are used as available.'[76] The two central cross-laths are first of
all bent up and the seat, usually of red pine or some other light
softwood, is inserted. The gunwale is then plaited with two
plaits above and below the seat. The remainder of the ash laths
are then bent and inserted in the gunwale. To make the
gunwale, hazel rods 8 feet long and as 'thick as a finger' are
required and about 45 rods of peeled hazel are required in order
to make the gunwale of one coracle. These are placed in water

for three or four days before plaiting. The wattled gunwale of a Towy coracle consists of three distinct lines of wattling, but the final, wattled plait is not inserted until the coracle maker is perfectly satisfied with the shape of the framing.

William Elias, Carmarthen.

Five yards of unbleached calico is required to cover the frame *(ofel)* of a Towy coracle. This is cut to shape, usually a woman's task, and the calico is sewn onto the frame, ensuring that the cover is taut. On a sunny day, the coracle is tarred and a leather strap for carrying is inserted in the seat.

Unlike the Teifi coracle, the Towy is equipped with a shallow turned wooden baler, required for work in a broad tidal estuary where the water can be rough and broken. The Towy coracle paddle is exceptionally long 'measuring overall 6 feet 1½ inches. The blade, including the well-sloped shoulder, is 2 feet 6 inches long, the loom 3 feet 7½ inches. The sides of the blade are parallel; in section it is slightly bi-convex. The loom is cylindrical in section and of equal diameter throughout; it is without either crutch or knob at the fore end'.[77] Paddles are made of either oak or ash, oak being preferred. The wooden club or *cnocer* up to 15 inches long is usually made of pitch pine, which many Carmarthen netsmen prefer to box-wood which is considerably harder and likely to spoil the appearance of a salmon. The *cnocer* and baler are carried under leather bands on the seat. A Carmarthen coracle is expected to last for at least four fishing seasons, but regular pitching is essential. Sometimes the upper plait of the woven gunwale has to be replaced, perhaps after two years, a process known as *ail godi* (re-raising). At the end of its useful life, it is customary to burn the coracle on the river bank.

On the Towy it is customary for fishermen to supply their children with miniature coracles. 'When I was nine or ten years of age', said one informant,[78] 'I was allowed out on the river in my own coracle, a rope was tied around me and the seat of my coracle and this was attached to my father's coracle. I was taught how to paddle with a stroke similar to a figure eight. As

I grew, I was given a larger coracle every year until I was fourteen or fifteen years of age, when I was given a full-sized coracle.'

Fishing on the Towy is carried out at night, the beginning of a fishing session at twilight being described as *clyfwchwr*. On a cloudless night as soon as 'seven stars appear in the sky' fishing can begin. The area fished consists of a large number of pools from the pump house near the old Carmarthen railway station to near the estuary. A trawl always begins nearer the right-hand bank of the river, described as *Ochor Tir* (the land side) rather than near the other bank of the river. At the end of a trawl the fishermen walk back to the starting point on the *ochor tir* side of the river, due to the large number of rivulets or 'pills' that enter the Towy on the left bank. As on the Teifi, the river is divided into a number of casts with a series of well-established fishing pools between Carmarthen Bridge *(Bont Gaer)* and the sea. The principal ones are:

Tinworks or Pump House (Upper Limit), Cerrig, Cerrig, Pwll-y-Baw, Gwar Ddarwen, [79] Towy Cottage, Pen-y-Morfa, Pil-y-Cathe, Bloiant, Pil-y-Dwrgwns, Brig-y-Brickyard, Towyside, Pwll-y-Bont, (Old Road Bridge), (Quayside), Myneni, [80] Llefach, Pwll-y-Gas, (New Road Bridge), Llyn Howell, Pwll-y-Bont, Gwar Pil-offi, Pil-offi, [83] (Johnstown Brook), Dwfnde, (White Bridge), Pwll Stafell, Gwar Stafell, Bwlch Gwaruchaf, Gwarisaf, Llyngoy, Brig y Bwtri, Bwtri, (Cook's Bank), Cornel, Gwar Gwter, Pwll Jinnieban ('Bwtchin y Ban'), Gwar Garw, (Carmarthen Sewage Outlet Llanstephan Rd), Gwar Garw, (River Pibwr), Gwar Uchaf, Pwll Du, (Long Reach), Pwll Du, (Green Castle Corner, Llanstephan Rd), Gwar Uchaf, Pwll Du, Gwar Gored, [81]

Gwar Tom, Bill Rees's Blocyn, Coch y Barlais, (Marsh), Penyclun, (Marsh), The Parrogs, (Lower Limit), Allt y Warddon, Banc yr Alma.[82]

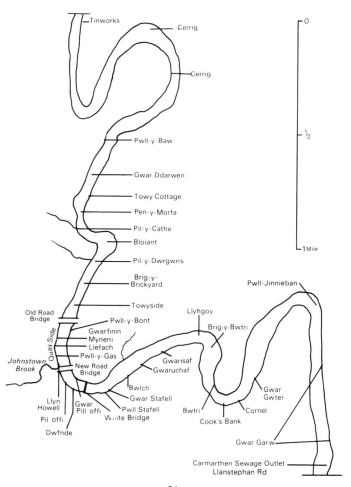

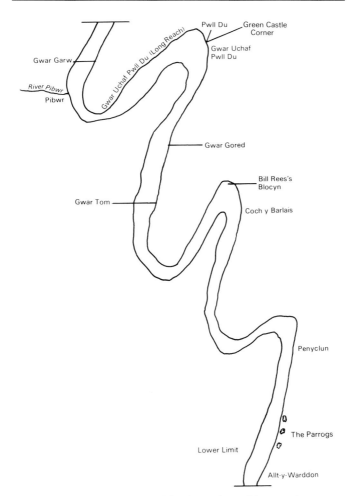

*Charts showing the extent of the salmon and sewin fishing grounds
of Carmarthen coracle fishermen.*

Cilgerran coracle fishermen, steel engraving.

Not all the casts that were used in the past are used today and the starting points are usually limited to Llyn Goy, Llyn Hywel Gwarfinen and Llyn Fach. The rigid rules of privilege and precedence, so apparent amongst the coracle men of Cenarth, Aber-cuch, Llechryd and Cilgerran, were always as well developed at Carmarthen. The first pair of coracles on the river bank with a net in place inside one of them is the first to begin the trawl. It is important that the net be inside the coracle or the

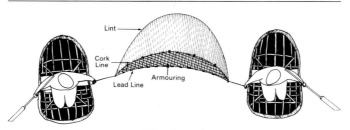

Fishing the coracle.

pair will forfeit their turn. After the first pair has drifted with the ebb tide 'to meet the fish' that swim upstream, for about 200 yards, or in line with a pre-determined landmark on the river bank such as a certain tree or rock, one of the coracle men beats his knocker against the side of his craft. This is a signal for the second pair of coracles in the queue on the river bank to enter the water. In the past, it was considered wrong for the coracle men to talk when they drifted, but as soon as a fish hit the net, a shout of '*na fe na fe*' ('there he is, there he is') would come from one of the fishermen, and the pair of coracles would be hauled rapidly towards one another. The salmon is knocked on the head and placed in the box under the seat. Before 1939 it was considered unlucky to hide a salmon on the river bank while the coracle men continued to fish, and it was not unusual for a coracle to carry as much as 80 pounds of salmon while the fishing continued. Today, however, a caught salmon is usually hidden on the river bank for collection later.

In hauling in a net, the partner nearest to the fish is responsible for hauling in the net into his coracle and moving rapidly towards his partner. The left-hand partner usually, but not invariably, holds the reeving line and stapling line in his right hand and many fishermen have preferences as to whether they occupy the left—or right-hand positions. One fisherman, for example, says, 'I've always fished with my left hand and I am completely deaf in my right, for I can never feel a fish with it. If my partner is also used to fishing with the left hand, I have to drift downstream with my back towards my partner, so that I can hold the net in my left hand.'[84]

A fishing session on the Towy extends from dusk to dawn, the session usually ending around 4 am. The Towy is regarded as a good river for sewin. In 1969, for example, the coracle men landed 1,470 sewin compared with 257 salmon.[85] So important is the sewin on the Towy that specific names are used to denote the weight of fish caught. A sewin weighing 3lb to 20lb is described as a *gwencyn*; a *twlpyn* weighs from 2lb to 3lb, while a sewin of less than 2lb is described as a *shinglin*.

1903, Carmarthen: left Dai Lewis, Dai 'Bigwn' Thomas; standing facing centre Jack Lewis; Right 'Billy Boy' Owens.

Postcard postmarked 1939. Note shipping and WCA warehouse.

The Towy Coracle Net

Although the Towy coracle net is similar in general design and method of usage to that of the Teifi, there are many differences in detail. If the Towy net is set off balance it will not fish properly so, says one coracle fisherman,[40] 'the arithmetic must be right. Generally speaking the bottom of the armouring is set in by the third and the head of the armouring slightly less than the third. The lint is set slightly less than the half.'

In the preparation of a coracle net the lines, made of cow's tail hair, have to be prepared first. The process of preparing these is exactly the same as that adopted by Teifi coracle men, with the exception that cow hair is used on the Towy instead of the horse hair of the Teifi. The head line *(carn ffun)*, the reeving line *(traill ffun)*, the foot line *(plwm ffun ucha)* and the hand line *(llaw ffun)* are made of three-ply strands while the second lead line *(plwm ffun isha)* is a two-ply strand. The hair is cut from a cow's tail and the longer the hair strands, the better. After it is thoroughly washed and picked, the unwanted hairs being disposed of, the resulting bunch of hair is placed in a shallow pan of water and covered with a heavy weight. After being steeped in water for some time, the hair is then spun into a single-ply rope, no more than an eighth of an inch in diameter. To do this a wooden rope twister *(trwc)* is used, and after about fifteen fathoms of single-ply rope has been spun, this is transferred to a second rectangular *trwc*. 'The single-ply rope', says Raymond Rees, a Carmarthen fisherman, 'is folded in half at the 30 yard mark and this end transferred to a third *trwc*. Spinning can now commence to form a two-ply rope. At the end of the original measured length, the rope is again folded and the work is completed to form the third ply. This is a three-man job and a set of *ffuniau* for a coracle net usually takes about ten days to complete.' All the ropes are made of dark brown or black hair, with the exception of the hand and reeving lines, which are invariably plaited from grey or white hairs. When fishing at night, it is important to distinguish one line from the other. The natural oils in cow hair give the lines their water-resistant qualities and prevent undue shrinkage. The amount of twist incorporated in the construction of a line prevents stretching, and gives it its strength; although the cow hair lines are very strong, they can be broken if the net, especially the foot line, gets caught up in debris on the river bottom. This particular quality is paramount if the net is to be saved, although with the recent advent of synthetic materials, the main lines are so strong that the net has to be cut from its obstruction and the net is usually a write-off.

With all the *ffuniau* of cow hair made, the next step in the construction of a net is the preparation of the lint. The size of mesh depends on the time of season. During the early months of March and April the lint mesh size is 4½ inches made of thick linen thread, size 10/3 or Number 53 nylon. During May and June, the fish begin to run smaller and a mesh of 3¾ inches is required. This is made of 12/3 linen thread or Number 43 nylon. In July and August, small sewin appear and the lint with a 3 inch mesh is made of 18/3 linen thread or Number 33 nylon. This type of fine meshed net is known as a *Gwangrwyd*. Carmarthen coracle fishermen are unwilling to use fine-meshed nets before the run of lampreys is over towards the middle of June. A fisherman using a large meshed net knows when to change to a finer one because 'he feels the fish going through the coarse meshed net of the early season'. As on the Teifi, the senior partner in a pair occupies the left-hand side of the river when fishing. Under the new legislation (1987) the licensee must always be present. Any two members of a team may fish as long as they carry a brass tag bearing the licence number on the net. Each team may possess two or three nets of each size, and one net may be used for fishing every night until it fails to catch a fish on a particular night. It is then customary to substitute another net, until it too fails to catch a fish.

In making a net of 3 inch mesh in linen or hemp, the lint is braided to 340 meshes wide and 34 meshes deep. After completion it is shrunk in hot and cold water and then measured to ensure that four full meshes measure not less then 12 inches (ie 4 x 3 inches). Assuming that the four meshes measure 12 inches, then the armouring can be made. The mesh size of the armouring is dependent on the lint and it must always be ¾ inches less than four meshes of lint. Therefore, the armouring must have a mesh of 11¼ inches from knot to knot. The length and depth of the armouring is also dependent on the lint. Since four lint meshes are equal to one armour mesh, then the lint length (320 meshes), divided by 4, equals the length of the armour, that is 80 meshes. The depth of the armouring is again determined by the lint, since the lint must be three times the depth of the armouring. It has been found by experiment that the best net is constructed 4½ meshes deep, each mesh being 11¼ inches which is within the legal maximum for depth.

The thread used to construct the armouring is usually much thicker than that used for the lint, being of 6/4 linen thread or Number 90 nylon.

The lint is now attached to the third half mesh from the head of the armouring, using a thin marrying linen thread. Four lint meshes are fixed in a continuing series of loops to each of the armour meshes until all 320 lint meshes are equally distributed in fours to the 80 armour meshes. These loops are called the *cwplins* (marryings). The next step is to complete the bag of the net by fixing it to the foot line. Rees describes the process as follows: 'To enable the armouring to hang in its correct proportions, that is by the third, it must evenly and accurately be set on the foot-rope *(plwm ffun ucha)*. Two full meshes of armouring (2 x 11¼) are divided by three and that measurement (7½ inches) is the division length between each armour length on the footline. Each one of these divisions is known as a *machogyn*. The second lead line *(plwm ffun isha)* is now attached to the first lead line and the bottom lint meshes evenly distributed in fours along its length. The side of the net are then sewn down to form the complete bag of the net.'

Because the net is drawn through the water in an arc, the foot line, if the net is to work properly, must be longer than the cork line. The difference in length is known as a *moilad*. 'It has been calculated', says Rees, 'that for every 20 *machogyns* on the foot-line the cork line must be 1½ *machogyns* shorter, thus on a net 80 *machogyns* long, 80 ÷ 20 = 4; 4 x 1½ = the *moilad* or 6 *machogyns* difference in length.' This figure is agreed by all to be the most important measurement in the coracle net. As each *machogyn* is 7½ inches apart, the cork line must be 6 x 7½ shorter (ie 45½ inches). The cork line fully stretched is 43 feet, but because of the arc when fishing, this is reduced to less than 33 feet and well inside the legal limit.

Unlike the Teifi coracle net, the Towy carries a line of corks and the setting of them is a complex process. Five 2 inch corks are evenly distributed between 10 cow's-horn rings on the cork line. The setting begins with fixing horn rings, followed by a cork, then a horn ring, then a cork and so on, with horn rings at the end of the line (see pp. 14 and 44).

The armour meshes are now hung between the series of corks and horns, and always hung in the same pattern—5, 5, 6, 6, 6, 6, 6; 6, 6, 6, 6, 6, 5, 5 = 80 meshes. It will be possible for a coracle net to be lengthened or shortened by six meshes, provided a horn ring and a cork is also added or subtracted. The ring at one end of the net is made fast to the *traill-ffun*; the other end ring is free to slide and close the net, rather like a purse string. To each of the end rings is made fast a *llaw-ffun*.

The net is now complete with the exception of being weighted with lead weights to ensure that the net fishes the bottom of the river efficiently. It is important among the Towy fishermen that these weights are of equal thickness, dimensions and weight, and the haphazard weighting practised by Teifi fishermen is not for the Carmarthen coracle man. Weights measure 1 inch by ¾ inches thick and weigh 5 or 6 grammes. They are hand made on a pair of stone moulds 6 inches long by 4 inches wide, in which two grooves 1 inch wide are cut. The lead is melted and run into the grooves in the stone. On cooling, lead strips of even thickness are produced, and these can be easily cut to the required sizes. When leading a net, account must be taken of the flow of the river, and weights are added or subtracted accordingly. Apart from flood water, tidal flows have to be considered and each fisherman has his own particular method to enable him to decide on how much water is flowing in the river at any one time. Stone steps, bridges, quarries, even grass banks may all give a key to the flow of the river, and a net has to be weighted according to the fisherman's judgement. Again, says Rees, 'The system of weighting adopted at Carmarthen is based on mathematics. Weighting always begins at the dead centre of the *plwm ffun*, that is on the fortieth *machogyn*. A single piece of lead is wound around both *plwm-ffuniau*, and working from the centre a piece of lead is fixed on the right hand side of the mesh to the right of the middle. Another lead weight is fitted on the left side of the mesh to the left of the middle of the net. In the dark, one knows exactly which side is which when fishing. Weighting is continued on both sides from the middle until the ends or *âls* are reached. As the *âls* will be close to the coracle, more weights are fixed to the ends than to the middle of the net, to allow for the extra drag.'

Accurate weighting of the net has always been the biggest problem for coracle fishermen and many a net has been discarded as being 'off balance', when in fact incorrect weighting has contributed to its failure. 'When I began fishing', continues Raymond Rees, 'it was generally accepted that one learnt the leading system parrot fashion, and it was only after careful study that a pattern appeared in the system, and praise must go to the designer of that system, whether by luck or judgement . . . for he concluded, whoever he was, that if two pieces of lead were placed side by side on the ends, then they should be followed by four single pieces. If three pieces were placed side by side then they should be followed by six double pieces followed by eight single pieces of lead. As the weight of lead in the *âls* increases, then a balance must be maintained towards the middle. If one fisherman asked how much water was flowing, he would not be answered ''6 to 8 inches'' but by the number of pieces of lead weight on his net and always in Welsh. For example, he would be answered in ascending order any one of the following: *dau-ddau* (two twos); *tri-dau* (three twos); *pedwar-dau* (four twos); *un-tri: pedwar-dau* (one three: four twos); *dau-tri: pump-dau* (two threes: five twos) etc.

Postcard postmarked 1910, Carmarthen. Note miniature paddles.

'Each side of the net is weighted separately and by experience it has been found that the left hand side is usually a few weights lighter. If, for example, a net is weighted on the right side *un-tri; pedwar-dau* it would contain 1 x 3, 4 x 2, 6 x 1, blank, one and so on to the middle of the net. The left side would contain 1 x 3, 3 x 2, 5 x 1, blank, one, blank and so on to the middle. As the flow of water increases, the blanks to the middle are filled: first forming a series of three single leads, then seven. All the blanks are taken up as in *unau* (ones) after which on every seventh a double is added as in *saith a dau* (7 x 2) and finally on every third a double weighting *tri a dau* (3 x 2). The *âls* or wings are leaded, the nomenclature of the various leadings being given as follows:

1 x 2: 3 x 1 *un a pob yn ail* through the net
2 x 2: 4 x 1 *un a pob yn ail* through the net
3 x 2: 5 x 1 *un a pob yn ail* through the net
4 x 2: 6 x 1 *un a pob yn ail* through the net
1 x 3: 4 x 2: 6 x 1 - *once tri a dim* through the net
2 x 3: 5 x 2: 7 x 1 - *twice tri a dim* through the net
3 x 3: 6 x 2: 8 x 1 - *3 times tri un a dim* through the net
4 x 3: 7 x 2: 9 x 1 - *4 times tri un a dim* through the net
1 x 4: 5 x 3: 7 x 2 - *tri-un-a-dim* through the net
2 x 4: 6 x 3: 9 x 2 - *full un a dim* through the net
3 x 4: 7 x 3: 10 x 2 - *full una dwy* through the net
4 x 4: 8 x 3: 11 x 2 - *full saith a dwy* through the net

'Of course the ends of the net can be made lighter by subtraction and corresponding subtraction from the middle, but that is where the experience and knowledge of river conditions come in.

William Elias.

'I have looked closely at the Towy and the Taf net and re-designed it. It took me ten years to design this new net which at last conforms with the Water Authority's regulations. The main differences are that the walling now conforms in the respect that it is now 22 inches around the four sides, the slackness is different and its overall length is within the

Dai Bigwn.

permitted limits of forty feet. The truth of the matter is that hitherto we were working with nets that, strictly speaking, were illegal.' The setting of the Towy net is by far the most

Wil y Dŵr.

complex of all, for as far as can be ascertained, complicated mathematical formulae never entered the calculations of coracle fishermen on other rivers. It is interesting to note that, although many Carmarthen coracle men like Raymond Rees are not Welsh speaking, their terminology and fishing nomenclature is always in the Welsh language and the persistence of fishing terms, probably from medieval Welsh, may be an indication of the antiquity of the coracle and the coracle net, on the Towy in particular.

FOOTNOTES

40. Raymond Rees, Carmarthen.

64. The licence fee for a Towy in 1972 was £12.00 with endorsee at 1 shilling each. On the Teifi coracle licences cost £15.37½p with 1 shilling endorsement.

65. Fishery Bye-Laws state 'A coracle net may be used . . . in the River Towy between an imaginary line drawn straight across the said river true north from a signal post adjacent to the main railway 241.25 miles (or thereabouts) from London and an imaginary line drawn straight across the said river from the Railway Pumping Station near the old Carmarthen Tin plate works'.

66. Hornell, *op, cit*, p 30, states that the following number of coracle licences were issued: 1929—25; 1930—22; 1931—23; 1932—19; 1934—19; 1935—13.

67. *Royal Commission, op, cit*, p 105.

68. Donovan, E: *Descriptive Excursions through south Wales and Monmouthshire* (1805), 2, p 227.

69. Wyndham, H P: *A Tour through Monmouthshire and Wales* (1781), p 52.

70. Evans, J: *Tour through South Wales* (1804), p 112.

71. *Second Report, op, cit*, (1863), p 22.

72. *Reports on Education in Wales* (HMSO 1847).

73. Williams, D: *The Rebecca Riots* (Cardiff 1953), p 51.

74. Hornell, *op, cit*, p 37.

75. *Ibid* p 33.

76. *Ibid* p 36.

77. *Ibid* p 34.

78. Robert Thomas: Welsh Folk Museum Record 3292 Car.

79. *Gwar* the neck of a pool.

80. *Meinen*—a rock on the river bed where nets can be caught (plural—*myneni*).

81. *Gored*—Fish weir.

82. Where the Carmarthen coracle men and Ferryside long netsmen fought in the 1850's.

83. *Pil*—a tidal rivulet.

84. Robert Thomas.

85. (South West Wales River Authority Report (1970), p. 47). See also p. 87.

Chapter 5

Coracle terms used by fishermen on Teifi and Towy

AL (Towy)—the heavily leaded wings or selvage of a net.

ASEN, pl *EISAU*, *EISE* (Teifi), *ISE* (Towy)—the ribs or laths of a coracle.

ASEN SAETHU (Towy)—the two main cross ribs or laths of a coracle.

ASTELL ORLES (ORLAIS) (Towy)—the plank, usually of light timber, at right angles to the seat, supporting it and forming a box for the catch.

BACHYN (Towy)—a forked stick for holding down the lath framing of coracles during construction.

Y BLETH (Teifi)—plaited hazel gunwale of coracle, *cf PLETH FAWR* (Towy).

BREST Y CORWG (Towy)—front of coracle, *cf BLA'N Y CORWG* (Teifi).

BLWMFFUN (Teifi)—leaded foot rope of a net, *cf PLWM-FFUN* (Towy).

BWRW (Teifi)—a cast, ie a stretch of river; *PEN-BWRW*—the starting point of a cast.

CARNFFUN, GARFFUN (Towy)—head-rope of a coracle net (*carn* [horn] + *ffun* [line]), *cf FFENEST-FFUN* (Teifi).

CLAWR (Towy)—a net mesh guage, *cf PREN MAGAL* (Teifi).

Y CEFEN (Teifi and Towy)—the lint of a coracle net.

CLYFWCHWR (Towy)—the time to begin fishing, ie twilight.

CNOCER (Teifi and Towy)—knocker or priest for killing salmon, *cf MOLLY KNOCKER* of lower Severn (molly / Severn name for salmon), occasionally on Teifi the *cnocer* is referred to as *PREN PYSGOD* (fish stick).

CWRWGL, CWRWG, CORWG (Teifi and Towy)—a coracle.

CWT Y CORWG (Teifi and Towy)—the rear of a coracle.

DELLTO (Teifi)—splitting laths for coracle frame.

DREI-FFUN (Towy)—reeving line, *cf FFUN FOWR* (Teifi).

EISE CROS (Teifi), *ISE CROS* (Towy)—cross laths.

EISE DANDRAD—ribs under the feet.

EISE HYD (Teifi)—longitudinal laths of a coracle, *cf ISE HIR* (Towy).

FADDUG (Towy)—the V-shape of meshes on head-rope and foot-rope.

FFENEST-FFUN (Teifi)—head rope of net, *cf CARN FFUN* (Towy).

FFIOL (Towy)—wooden baler, not used on Teifi.

FFUN, pl *FFUNIAU* (Teifi and Towy)—the main rope of a net.

FFUNEN (Teifi)—fishing rod.

FFUN FOWR (Teifi)—reeving line, *cf DREI-FFUN* (Towy).

Y FRÂS (Teifi)—armouring of net, *cf RHWYD RÔTH* (Towy).

GAFEL (Teifi)—the claw *(gafael)* at the top of a Teifi coracle paddle.

GASEG (Teifi)—shaving horse used for shaping laths, not often used by Towy coracle builders.

Y GORON (Towy)—the spot where the two diagonal laths *(eise saethu)* cross one another.

Cilgerran coracle man c. 1910.

GWANGRWYD (Towy)—a fine meshed net of about 3 inches bar for use in catching large salmon and small sewin, down to 1lb in weight; mainly used at the end of the season.

GWAS (Teifi)—endorsee of coracle licence.

GWEDEN (YR WEDEN) (Teifi)—a twisted withy, hazel or oak sapling used for carrying coracle, *cf STRAPEN GWDDWG* (Towy).

GWE FRÂS (Teifi)—armouring of net.

GWRAGEN (Towy)—a lath loop around the front of the gunwale of a Towy coracle for the protection of the outside.

GWRHYD (Teifi mainly)—a measure of the length of a coracle net. *GWR* (man) + *HYD* (length), ie a measure of a man's outstretched arms.

HALA CWRWG (Teifi)—to be a coracle fisherman, literally 'to send a coracle'.

HELINGO (Teifi)—the process of covering a coracle.

LLAW FFUN (Towy)—stapling line (handline).

LLYGAD (Towy)—mesh, *cf MAGAL* (Towy and Teifi).

MACHOGYN (Towy)—the gap between meshes of a net on *PLWM-FFUN*; for every 20 *machogyn* on the lead line, the cork line must be 1½ *machogyns* shorter.

MAGAL, pl MAGLE (Towy and Teifi)—mesh of net.

MAGLE BACH (Teifi)—lint of coracle net.

MAGLE MOWR (Teifi)—armour of a coracle net.

MOELYD NOL (Towy)—to go back to the beginning of a trawl or pool by paddling the coracle rather than carrying it.

MOILAD (Towy)—the difference between the length of cork line and lead line; to much *moilad* will mean that each mesh is elongated; too little *moilad* means that the meshes are stretched horizontally.

OFEL (Towy)—frame of a coracle.
ORAGE (Teifi)—frame of a coracle.

PLETH FACH (Teifi)—withy plait that runs from the gunwale and along the bottom of a Teifi coracle to give added strength at the back.
PLETH FAWR (Toey)—wattled gunwale, *cf Y BLETH* or *Y BLETH DOP* (Teifi).
PITCHO CORWG (Teifi and Towy)—to put pitch on a coracle; referred to occasionally as *RHOI COFOR* (putting on a cover).
PREN MAGAL (Teifi)—a net mesh gauge, *cf CLAWR* (Towy).
PLWM-FFUN (Towy)—leaded foot rope of a coracle net. *Plem-ffun ucha*—upper lead line attached to lint—three-ply cow-hair ropes; *Plwm-ffun isha*—lower lead line attached to armouring every third mesh—two-ply cow-hair rope.
PWYLLO'R FFUNIAU (a) arranging the rope and nets in a coracle (Towy); (b) the bunching of the net meshes together when a fish is caught (Teifi).

RHAWN—horse hair (Teifi) or cow hair (Towy) used in making coracle net ropes.
RHWYD FÂN (Towy)—lint of coracle net.
RHWYD RÔTH (Toey)—armouring of a coracle net.

SDOL (Teifi)—ie stool—coracle seat, *cf AQÉT* (Towy).
STRAPEN CNOCER (Towy)—strap to hold knocker in place on seat.
STRAPEN FFIOL (Towy)—strap holding baler in place.
STRAPEN GWDDWG (Towy)—the ash or leather carrying strap, *cf GWDEN* (Teifi), also *STRAPEN CWRWG*.

TEIRCAIN (ie *TRI* [three] + *CAIN* [hank])—the three-ply horse- hair (Teifi) or cow-hair (Towy) of the *ffenest-ffun* (headrope) and *plwm-ffun* (lead line).

TRAILL-FFUN (Teifi)—stapling line carrying horn rings.

TRYC, TRWC (Towy)—a rope twister, somewhat similar to that used in making straw rope for making the *ffuniau* (ropes) of a coracle net.

WAL (Towy)—lint of a net, *cf Y CEFEN, RHWYD FAWR* (Teifi).

WECHAIN (ie *CHWECH* [six] + *CAIN* [hank])—six-ply of horse hair (Teifi) or cow hair (Towy) of the *ffun-fowr* (reeving line).

YSGAR (Towy)—half a mesh.

YSGAR Y GATH—the lowest line of meshes in a net, usually on the armouring; this must be large enough for a salmon to get through to the lint beyond.

Towy coracle men at Mumbles regatta: Dai Loggles, Wil y Dŵr, Yankee.

Chapter 6

The Tâf Coracle

The Tâf is a short river, 32 miles long, that runs into the sea at Carmarthen Bay. One pair of coracles is licensed to fish in the lower tidal portion of the river 'between an imaginary line drawn straight across the said river from Whaley Point to Ginst Point and the main road bridge spanning the said river situate one mile or thereabouts below St Clears'.[85] The coracle men are all part-time fishermen based on the village of Lower St Clears. Although the fishermen are allowed to fish as far as the estuary of the river near Laugharne, most of the fishing is done between the two bridges at St Clears. In an enquiry, where it was proposed to change the boundary of coracle fishing in 1971, one witness complained of 'the operation of coracle nets in the River Tâf, between the two bridges. The river there is very narrow and when the coracles are fishing not much space is left for fish to move upstream. The area for coracle fishing extends a long way downstream of the lower bridge and I do not know of any reason why the coracles could not fish in that stretch. During the last few years coracle netsmen have fished very regularly and have had good catches. Their use of motor cars as transport from one bridge to another has meant that they have been able to carry out a large number of sweeps daily.'[86]

It was maintained at this enquiry that the bye-law relating to the limits of coracle fishing was ambiguous for the river authority believed that 'the upper limit is meant to be the A4066 bridge approximately one mile directly south of St Clears' but the coracle netsmen 'have claimed that the upper limit is the A477 bridge approximately one mile south-west of St. Clears'. As a result of this ambiguity, the Tâf fishermen fished mainly in a stretch of river approximately one mile long between the two road bridges: a stretch of river considered totally unsuitable for the operation of coracles by the authorities. 'This stretch is at the upper limit of the tide and the channel of this small river is only 20 to 25 feet wide in places. Thus, when the net is fishing, few fish can move upstream because the net is across a substantial portion of the river. In addition particularly during low flows, sea trout stay in this stretch of river for long periods when a large proportion are caught by the coracle nets.'[87]

In evidence submitted by the coracle fishermen it was stated:

'There are two bridges in St Clears, both crossing the river Tâf, and it has at all times been accepted by the Licensing Authority and the Netsmen, that the said description applies to the higher bridge, that is to say the bridge directly below and a mile or thereabouts from St Clears on the A477.

'If a ruling was given that the bridge so defined in the existing bye-law was the second bridge crossing the River Tâf on the A4066 which has never been accepted by anyone concerned, it would in practice be tantamount to total prohibition of net fishing on the River Tâf. This is evidenced by the fact that the river can be properly approached on its stretch below the higher bridge by public right of way, but river access would be prohibited if the lower bridge was defined as the commencement of the fishing length as it is bounded on both banks by privately owned land which could prohibit passage by trespass. To realistically appreciate the position, it must be understood that the only fishable stretch of the present length is that part of the river lying between the two bridges. Below the second bridge the river bed is obstructed with tree stumps, weed growth, deep slime, and the adjoining marshes

Edgeworth Evans.

interlaced with deep wide drainage gulleys making coracle drift netting down stream and the consequent walk back an impossibility and beyond this, the length nears the river bar. It is clear, therefore, that to define the second bridge as the starting point of the permitted length is nothing more or less than total net prohibition and in that sense would be a ruling in excess of the powers of purely limitation order. When the limitation order restricting net fishing was introduced in 1931, it received the full co-operation of netsmen and their endorsees, and thus in a measure these very ancient fishing skills were preserved. It would therefore be a breach of faith on the part of the fishery constitution to so vary a bye-law as in effect to totally prohibit coracle net fishing in this area, which has already accepted the preservation of this ancient rural craft by a limitation order which insures practical continuance of coracle net fishing by the yearly issue of two licences only.

'At the Public Enquiry convened in 1971, the Inspector in his report recommended that the upper limit be the road bridge crossing the A 477 (Tenby road).'

Until 1987 the number of coracles on the Tâf has remained constant since 1935, two pairs being licensed at that time. In 1933 three coracle nets were licensed, but in the eighteen-sixties 'between 40 and 50' were employed in salmon fishing on the Tâf.[88] Earlier in the century a traveller to South Wales, Donovan[89] saw at St Clears 'a number of the poor inhabitants of the neighbouring cottages eagerly pursuing their customary occupations in the coracle fishery'. Donovan, although he had seen many coracles at Carmarthen, was particularly impressed by 'those feats of dexterity which are required in the management of such a capricious vessel' which characterized the coracle men of the Tâf, or the 'Corran' as he called the river.

Although St Clears is no more than eight miles from Carmarthen, and although the Tâf has a common estuary with the Towy, the Tâf coracles have suffered considerable modifications to suit the configuration of the river. Although the Tâf coracle is similar in general shape of the Towy, it is considerably heavier than the Carmarthen coracle. The front is flatter and the back more pointed and the wattled gunwale of the Towy is replaced by planking. When Hornell carried out his survey in the nineteen-thirties he described the Tâf coracle as follows.[90] 'The lattice part of the framework consists of seven longitudinal frames interlaced with either five or six transverse ones, all made of rough laths 1¼ and 1½ inches wide. No diagonal laths are present, but two or three short accessory laths to strengthen the bottom under the feet may be intercalated with several of the foremost transverse frames. The end of all the frames, bent up in the usual manner, are inserted, after being whittled down to cylindrical points about ⅜ inch in diameter into vertical holes made at intervals in a broad gunwale frame of thin board; this takes the place of the wattled gunwale of the Teifi and Towy coracles . . . The seat is set flush with this gunwale, cleats below joining it to the gunwale frame, which does not extend beneath the seat. The partition supporting the after border of the seat is made of a number of broad strips of thin board set vertically at short intervals apart. These are nailed below to a basal bar extending across the bottom, while above they are nailed to a long cleat screwed to the underside of the seat. The cover is of calico coated with a mixture made by boiling 1lb of pitch with 1½lb of Stockholm tar. A round drainage hole is cut in the cover at the tail end, high up for the easy emptying of water when the coracle is taken out of the river.'

More recent examples of Tâf coracles resemble the Towy type although measurements and proportions are slightly different. An example made in 1970 and now at the Welsh Folk Museum consists of seven longitudinal and seven cross laths, the latter being all in front of the seat. Behind the seat to the slightly pointed back of the coracle there are no cross laths. Unlike pre-war coracles, the present day ones are equipped with two diagonal braces that cross in front of the seat. The gunwale, like the body laths, is made up of two layers of ash, thickly pitched, 1½ inches deep with the tips of all the laths inserted between the two layers. Attached to the deal seat are a strap for carrying and another for holding the knocker in place. Three planks at right angles to the seat act as a carrying box, while the seat itself is merely nailed to the top of the gunwale and flush with it. In use, the fisherman has to sit well forward of the centre of the coracle to provide equilibrium, for on the ground the Tâf coracle has the appearance of being particularly lop-sided with the back almost touching the ground and the front rising at a sharp angle. The paddle is of the Towy type, 5 feet long with a blade 2 feet long with parallel sides and gently sloping shoulders. The knocker is of crab apple wood or box wood, and although a strap is provided for carrying it on the seat, by tradition Tâf coracle fishermen preferred to carry the club in their pockets.

It seems that considerable modification in the design of the Tâf coracle took place in the late nineteenth century, so that recent examples closely resemble those of the Towy. One informant said[91] that to build a Taf coracle of the older variety a naturally curving branch of a tree, usually an apple tree, was

Billy Beynon St. Clears 1937, Tâf coracle.

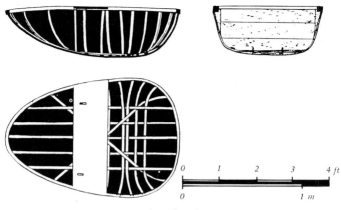

The Tâf coracle.

cut and split in half to form the fore-part of the gunwale. The two sections were fixed together with a cleat iron. Another branch was treated in the same way to form the rear gunwale. Unlike the Towy coracle, it was the gunwale of the Tâf coracle that was formed first and this was bored with a series of holes for receiving the laths of the coracle frame. Seven longitudinal and seven cross laths were prepared by cleaving willow with a froe. These were pointed, laid down on the floor and the pointed ends inserted in the hole in the gunwale. A seat was tacked on top of the gunwale and the coracle was covered and tarred in the usual manner.

The following are examples of the dimensions of two Taf coracles:

Coracle A was made by Edgeworth Evans of Lower St Clears in 1970, now at the Welsh Folk Museum (Accession Number F71-70). Coracle B was measured by Hornell in 1937[92]

	A	B
Overall length	59in	57in
Maximum width	39¾in	42in
Width at seat	39in	39in
Width at back	38in	37in
Depth (amidships)	18½in	Not given
Height (front)	5½in	Not given
Height (seat)	19in	12½in
Height (back)	15½in	Not given
Width of seat	11in	Not given
Weight	31lb	33lb

FOOTNOTES

85. *South West Wales River Authority Report* (1970), p 47.

86. *South West Wales River Authority. Proposed Fishery Bye-Laws* (unpublished 1971). Evidence of Bailiff Brian Morgan at Public Enquiry 14 January 1971.

87. *Ibid*. Evidence of Dr W Roscoe Howells, Water Authority and Fisheries Officer, South West Wales River Authority.

88. *Minutes of Evidence, op, cit*, (1861).

89. Donovan, *op, cit*, 2, p 228.

90. Hornell, *op, cit*, p 38.

91. R Rees.

92. Hornell, *op, cit*, p 40.

Chapter 7

Coracle Fishing
on Other Rivers

The use of the coracle as a fishing craft has declined very rapidly in recent years and today coracle fishing is limited to three rivers only, the Teifi, Towy and Taf in west Wales. In the nineteen-twenties and thirties, coracles were to be found on many other rivers such as the Dee, the Eastern Cleddau in Pembrokeshire and the Severn, while in the late nineteenth century other rivers such as the Wye, Usk, Conway, Dyfi, Nevern and Loughor had coracle fishermen. Each river had its own specific type of craft, but many examples have disappeared without a record being made of them.[93]

Cleddau

Coracle fishing persisted on the eastern branch of the Cleddau until 1939, when a single pair of coracles was licensed to fish. Even in the eighteen-sixties, the number of coracles on the Cleddau never exceeded 6 pairs above Llawhaden bridge, and 6 to 10 below.[94] The coracles were used frequently for poaching. By 1930, the number had declined to three and by 1934 one pair only was found on the river. Coracle fishing ceased completely in the early nineteen-forties.

The Cleddau coracle was closely related in type to that used on the Tâf and had 'the same short squat from; the same deep, wide, square fore end and short rounded ''tail'' as that of the Tâf. Clear evidence of its origin is afforded by the form and size of the paddle. This is 4 feet 3 inches long, made up of a short blade, 2 feet by 3¼ inches and a loom ending in a transverse claw grip, identical with that of the Teifi paddle'.[95]

The Cleddau coracle.

Although no Cleddau coracle has been preserved, it is possible to deduce details of its construction from photographs.[96] The framework of the coracle consists of six laths, made of sawn ash 1½ inches wide running the length of the coracle and nailed to the inner side of the planked gunwale. At right angles to these laths are inter-woven three cross laths, six in front of the seat to provide support for the fisherman's feet and two behind the seat. All the laths are bent upward and nailed to the gunwale. The gunwale itself consists of a lath, about 1½ inches wide, bent into a U-shape to form the sides and back of the coracle frame. Nailed to this is a piece of wood, approximately 1½ inches square, that forms the bow of the coracle. The front framing of the Cleddau coracle therefore is far more squared than that of the Teifi. Two diagonal laths that intersect beneath the seat completes the frame. The seat, with leather carrying strap and leather knocker strap, is placed midway along the length of the coracle. Two pieces of wood from about 14 inches to 18 inches long and about 1½ inches

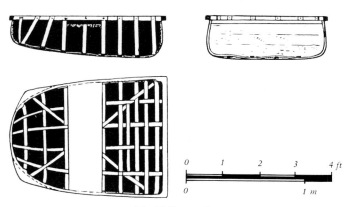

The Cleddau coracle.

square are bolted on either side of the seat to the gunwale. The deal seat in turn is bolted to the underside of these two pieces of wood. a solid bulkhead is screwed to the seat about 3 inches from the back end and this runs to the floor of the coracle being supported by the crossed diagonal laths of the framing. Hornell said that the Cleddau coracle was covered with Hessian canvas, coated with a mixture of pitch and tar. The measurements he gives are as follows:

Length—52 inches   Breadth—40 inches
Depth (front)—14 inches   Depth (amidships)—13 inches
Depth (back)—10 inches   Width of seat—12 inches

Usk and Wye

A coracle was last used for angling in the Usk around 1930, but undoubtedly coracle fishing was well known on the river and its tributaries as well as on Llangors Lake *(Llyn Safaddan)* until the late nineteenth century. In Camden's *Brittania*[97] of 1586 'Llyn Savaddan . . . In English 'tis called Brecknockmore . . . well stored with otters and also Perches, Tenches and Eels, which the Fishermen take in their coracles'.

It seems that although nets were used on the Wye and Usk for salmon fishing, the coracle was more widely used in angling. Sir John Hawkins in his 1760 edition of Izaak Walton's *Compleat Angler* for example[98] notes that 'the men of Monmouthshire made use of "a thing called a Thorrocle or Truckle" when fishing, in this case fly fishing for grayling, which were not easy to get at without a boat or wading. In some places it is called a "Coble", from the Latin "Corbula", a little basket; it is a basket shaped like the half of a walnut shell,

The Wye and Usk coracle.

but shallower in proportion and covered on the outside with a horse's hide; it has a bench in the middle and will just hold one person, and is so light that the countrymen will hang it on their heads like a hood, and so travel with a small paddle which serves for a stick till they come to a river; and then they launch it and step in: there is great difficulty into getting into one of those Truckles: for the instant you touch it with your foot, it flies from you, and when you are in, the least inclination of the body oversets it.'

A mid-nineteenth-century writer[99] noted that on the Usk 'many of the inhabitants gained their livelihood a great portion of the year by netting and angling. During the season, near the town of Usk, ten or a dozen fishermen were to be seen carrying their coracles on their backs in going to and returning from their avocation . . . Their shape resembled the section of a walnut shell, the length was about five feet and the breadth about four, with a seat placed across the centre; they were made of thin hoops crossed, with very strong basket work edges, and covered with strong coarse canvas thickly coated with pitch . . . the fisherman might often have been observed to work his paddle with one hand while he conducted the net with the other, at the same time holding a line in his teeth . . . On the banks of the Usk, Wye and other fresh water rivers, these coracles were to be seen hanging at the doors of many of the cottages'. After 16 July 1866 it became illegal to fish for salmon without a licence on the Usk[100] and each coracle licensee had to pay an annual fee of £2 to use a net in a fishing season that extended from 1 March to 31 August.

On the Wye and Monnow coracle fishing was also widely practised until about 1914, but after that date the number of coracles in use declined rapidly, and there is no evidence to suggest that coracles persisted after World War 1.[101] In the Ross area they were widely used in the nineteenth century. A traveller in 1799,[102] for example, noted that 'During the course of the navigation from Ross, we passed several small fishing craft called Truckles or Coricles, ribbed with laths or basketwork, and covered with pitched canvas.'

Down river at Monmouth they were equally well known. 'Many salmon are caught at this place which is five miles [upstream] from Monmouth' said one writer in 1805.[103] 'Here we saw several boats, called coricles, peculiar to this part of the river . . . we saw two men going out in their coricles to fish. Each man lays hold of one end of a net, about 20 yards long, and paddles down the river till they feel a strike. They then haul it up as quick as possible and draw it on shore. They paddle along at a great rate, and put us much in mind of what we read concerning the Indians in their canoes.'

The Wye and Usk coracle at Ross.

The fact that the Wye coracle fishermen used an armoured net is confirmed by a witness to the Royal Commission on Salmon Fisheries in 1861.[104] The mesh of net was 2½ inches and in addition to drifting with the flow of the stream, as in west Wales, Wye fishermen used coracles for the process of 'bushing'. A bush, a hole or rock in the river, was surrounded by a net and the salmon driven out of its hiding place by poking with a pole. For the more orthodox technique of drawing with a 'truckle net' a witness to the Commission said: 'There are two coracles apart from one another and about 16 yards of net. One man has a running line; each man holds one end of the net with one hand, and paddles with the other to keep the coracles as far apart as the net will allow: directly they feel a fish, the man at one end lets go and the other draws up and the fish is bagged and drawn into the coracle.'

As on the Usk, the use of the coracle for angling persisted longer than its use for netting on the Wye. One Ross angler 'used a reel, but others only had a large cork bung on a short piece of cord attached to the rod butt, and on hooking a fish, the lot was heaved overboard. The rod, etc, played the fish, and directly he rested the fisherman paddled after his bung and gave it a pull to start the quarry off again'.[105] Hornell describes the rod and line used for coracle fishing in the Hereford district.[106] 'The rod is of elm, short and stiff, and shaped like a billiard cue, tapering upward from a stout and heavy butt. Its length is barely 8 feet. The line is of horsehair, about 24 feet long, tapering from a diameter of 3mm down to six hairs at the end.'

The coracles used on the Usk and Wye were identical in construction and were usually constructed by the fishermen themselves. The Monmouthshire 'truckle', as it was called locally, showed a marked resemblance to those used on the

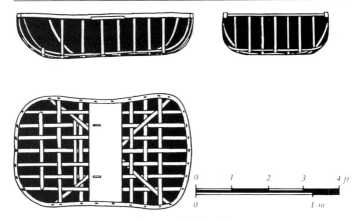

The Wye and Usk coracle.

Towy, which may suggest a common origin. It differs, however, in that the section behind the seat is longer than the section in front of the seat and the seat is not set near the centre as on Towy coracles. The gunwale of the Monmouthshire coracle has none of the sheer displayed by the Towy. An example of a Wye coracle preserved at the Hereford City Museum[107] and made by William Dew of Kerne Hill, Ross on Wye, about 1910, has a broad and deep fore-end and a rounded stem with the laths curving up gently at the back. The sides are parallel and the gunwale almost horizontal. The dimensions are as follows:

Length—60 ins.
Width (fore end)—39½ ins.
Width (at seat)—38 ins.
Width (back)—39 ins.
Width of seat—11 ins.

Height (fore end)—14½ ins.
Height (at seat)—14½ ins.
Height (stern)—15½ ins.
Weight—28lb

The coracle has seven longitudinal ash laths and six transverse laths, inserted in a woven hazel gunwale. Between the sixth and seventh cross lath and behind the seventh are two short accessory laths to give added strength in the long tail of the Wye coracle. A pair of diagonal laths cross just in front of the seat, giving added support to the solid bulkhead under the seat. A leather carrying strap is fitted.

The paddle of a Wye and Usk coracle is similar to that of a Towy, being 5 feet long and with a parallel-sided blade from 18 inches to 21 inches long. The loom is straight and cylindrical.

Hornell describes the method of building coracles adopted by Mr A C Morgan of Monmouth.[108]

'The framework consisted of seven longitudinal and seven, or rarely eight transverse laths crossing one another at right angles, with two diagonals, all arranged after the Towy fashion. When a coracle was to be begun Morgan states: ''I used to go to the sawyer and say 'Rip me out a set of laths'.'' These had to be split from willow logs [sally-wood]; sawn laths were not considered satisfactory, width 1¾ inches to 2 inches. These laths were soaked in water for two days before use. When judged pliable enough, they were laid on the ground and interlaced at the proper distances apart. Then the main crossing points were secured either by means of forked pegs driven into the ground [Carmarthen method] or were held down by weights [Cenarth method]. This done the ends of the laths were bent up and secured in position by plaiting withy bands around them at gunwale level. The ends of two of the transverse laths a little in front of mid-length were the first to be bent up; these were passed through slots in the ends of the seat. Amidships rigidity was obtained by inserting a solid deal partition of template form beneath the seat. This was tied below at two points to the lath framework and above at two corresponding points to the seat, the sewing passing through two small holes forward of each of the slots made for the carrying strap.

'The withy gunwale plaits were arranged in such a way that if a plait was begun on the left behind the seat and circled forward clockwise, the end of its half-circle had to finish on the right in front of the seat; the complemental semi-circle reversed this procedure—it started in front of the seat on the tight and then circled round the stern to end and interlock with the beginning of the fore-end plait, behind the seat on the left.'

A wooden mallet for killing the fish was carried, made preferably of apple or pear wood. A bailer was considered unnecessary.

The cover was of stout calico and was usually called the 'Hide' of the coracle. The fishermen's wives made the cover; after stretching it over the frame and lashing it on below the upper plait of the gunwale, a coating of a mixture of pitch and coal tar was applied on the outside. Afterwards the coracle was taken (in Monmouth) to the Gas Works and left in one of the retort houses for 24 hours in order that the mixture should thoroughly permeate the fabric of the cover. After being brought home, a second coating of the same mixture was applied. The mixture was carefully tested; a stick was dipped into it and brought out with a small blob of the stuff on its end. After a few seconds it was passed between the fingers and then, if it stretched and did not crack, it was considered to be of the right consistency.

Dee

In 1920 coracle netting rights on the Dee were bought out by the Dee Fishery Board, who since 1903 had made a conscious attempt to limit coracle netting by not issuing new licences on the death or retirement of a licensee. In 1920 the three remaining nets operating on the river in the Bangor-on-Dee— Overton district were bought out for £1,000, and as a result coracle netting on the river ceased. Nevertheless coracles remained in use for angling until the nineteen-fifties. 'A coracle is almost a necessity on the rough, rocky, middle reaches of the Dee', says one writer,[109] 'when owing to the force of the current and deep, hidden ledges, and clefts in the rocky bottom, wading is impossible in many places and no other type of craft, not even a birch bark canoe could possibly be used.'

In the nineteenth century, coracle netting was undoubtedly widely practised on the Dee, especially in the upper reaches of the river. One witness to the Commissioners on Salmon Fisheries in 1861, for example,[110] said 'It happened frequently that several hundreds of the men would go out very early in the morning with coracles on their backs, pass over the mountains and come some distance down the river, taking all they could catch with very fine nets. They all met at a certain public house, where large white baskets were filled with what they had obtained and sent to the Liverpool and Manchester markets.'

Even in the eighteen-sixties, coracles were a considerable source of worry to the authorities, for the 15 pairs that operated between Bangor and Erbistock weir were 'fished upon suffrance for many years'.[111] In 1862 says another report[112] 'The coracle fishing has been rather increased this year, and this mode of fishing somewhat endangers the future of the river

The Dee coracle.

. . . Unless some restriction be placed upon this class of fisherman, it is evident that they will increase as the fish increase . . . Complaints have been frequently made to us that the coracle fishing has discouraged the proprietors from taking steps to improve the river, because they would derive no benefit thereby, and increase what they already consider to be a nuisance'. During the last three decades of the nineteenth century, coracle netting was certainly discouraged on the Dee and whereas 27 licences for netting were taken out in 1871, by 1884 the number had decreased to 15 licences and by 1895 to 12. In addition, in 1888 the Fishery Board limited the length of the salmon fishing season by putting back the opening of the season from 1 February to 31 March, 'with the view of making certain that Kelts had a fair chance of returning to the sea'.

Although the coracle persisted on the Dee until fairly recently amongst anglers, it was hardly ever used in the nineteenth century for that purpose 'except for catching eels with a ''bob''—a bunch of worms upon worsted'.[113] In the nineteen-forties and fifties many of the coracles used by anglers, especially in the Llangollen district, were made to accommodate two persons and the vessels were wider than many of those used on the other rivers. Usually they were about 55 inches wide by 57 inches long. Oddly enough two-man coracles persisted longer and were more common on the Dee than the one-man variety, for as Hughes-Parry says: 'Most coracles are made to accommodate two persons, although a certain number of single coracles are still in use.'[114] These double coracles weighed about 40lb and with them 'it is possible to shoot rapids and dodge in between out-jutting ledges in the fastest and wildest stream, holding on by gaff and paddle to some outcropping ledge or rock; and one can tuck

Angling from a Dee coracle.

oneself in in perfect safety with a rush of wild white water on each side. By using a coracle one can therefore fish places that could never by reached either by wading or throwing the longest line from the bank'.

There were two distinct types of Dee coracle.

1. The Lower Dee coracle used mainly in the Bangor-Iscoed-Overton area.

2. The Upper Dee coracle used between Bala as far as beyond the mouth of Ceiriog. Most of these coracles were to be seen in the vicinity of Llangollen.

The Lower Dee coracle, an example of which is preserved at the Welsh Folk Museum, has sharp in-curving sides, especially below the seat, and a broad flattened bow with a more rounded stern. The framework is formed of interlaced ash laths, that are much thinner and narrower than those used in any other coracle type. There are nine of these longitudinal laths, each no more than ¾ inches wide, and these laths are strengthened by a number of supplementary laths that are inserted, one on each side of the five central splints, in front of the seat where the coracle fisherman's feet will rest. The transverse laths too are greatly increased in number and the majority are arranged in compound sets, each set corresponding to one of the broad transverse laths of south Wales coracles. The first of the transverse laths from the bow of the vessel consists of three separate splints, the second, four and the third, five. The gunwale is formed of two ash laths bent to shape with the deal seat inserted between the two, while the *cratch*, the box-like space under the seat, is formed by a stout pillar under the seat and lattice work. This cuts the coracle into two separate sections—a fore section 30 inches long and an after compartment 24 inches long.

When not in use the coracle is set upright upon its 'tail'. To prevent deformation of the slender framework when thus up-ended, a stout median wooden bar is inserted between the seat and the centre of the stern gunwale.

A paddle, a carrying strap of the usual type, and a thong loop passed around the central pillar below the seat are the only accessories. The paddle is 5 feet long and of unusual elegance. The blade and loom are of equal length; the blade tapers evenly from the broad distal end, and were it not for the merest trace of shouldering, would merge insensibly into the cylindrical loom. No crutch is present; in its place we find the end of the loom encircled by an iron band, notched or slotted at one side. When the owner slings the coracle on his back, he passes the end of the loom through the thong loop passed around the seat pillar; the notch serves to prevent the loop from slipping off.

The principal dimensions of a Lower Dee coracle from Overton are:

Length—55 inches
Length of seat—38 inches
Maximum width (front)—38 inches
Width of seat—11 inches
Maximum width (centre)—35 inches
Depth (at seat)—14 inches
Maximum width (back)—47 inches

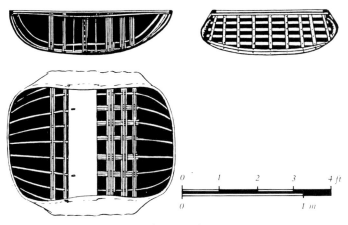

The Dee coracle.

Hornell describes the method of construction as follows:[115]

'The two sets of laths which are to form the framework are arranged as usual on the ground or preferably on a wooden flooring where they are kept in relative position after interlacing by weights or by tacking down.

'The ends of the transverse laths on one side are then bent up and locked between two stiff rods running longitudinally, each lath being tied to these two embracing rods. The lath ends on the opposite side are similarly treated; this done, the ends of the two opposed pairs of rods are connected by cords at the distance apart which is to be the eventual width of the coracle at gunwale level. The ends of the longitudinal laths are similarly treated and held in place by cords running fore and aft. The result is that the framework appears of the form of a rectangular basketwork trough with the four sides not joined together at the corners.

'To facilitate bending, the laths are sometimes thinned slightly at the bends.

'When the curved laths are considered to be sufficiently set, the latticework seat-partition is placed in position and wired at several points along the bottom edge to the laths below. This done the two lower gunwale hoops are nailed in position, one outer and the other inner to the laths and about an inch and a half below what will be the eventual gunwale edge. The ends of the laths embraced by the paired rods are now released and the seat may be put in, its ends passing over and beyond the lower gunwale hooping. The ends of three of the transverse laths are passed through slots in each end, a procedure which causes the waist-like appearance when the coracle is completed. The seat is further secured by being wired at intervals through paired holes to the upper edge of the partition below.

'The upper gunwale hoops are next added, one on each side of the projecting frame ends, which are now cut off flush. These upper hoops pass over the seat ends.

'The coracle is now ready to be covered with calico. The edges are reflected over the gunwale and tacked on. After receiving a coating of the usual pitch and tar mixture, and extra inner gunwale hoop is added to hide and protect the turned-in edge of the coracle.'

The Upper Dee coracle, used in the past from Bala Lake to below the mouth of the River Ceiriog, differs considerably from the type of coracle used in the Overton-Bangor districts. They were used until recently in the Llangollen district and most were designed to carry two people. For this reason the coracles were given a more accentuated bilge so that in appearance the Llangollen coracle was almost square, with the ends considerably sheered.

The Llangollen coracle differed from the Bangor-Overton type in that broad, planed laths were used for the frame construction. Nine of these were interlaced with sixteen transverse laths to form a stout framework that was further strengthened by the addition of four diagonal laths. Seven stout squared pillars inserted into cross-bars formed the cratch and support for the seat. Unlike the Lower Dee coracle, the Llangollen type did not possess the distinctly pinched waist, so characteristic of the coracle of Bangor and Overton. Methods of carrying also differed, for the Llangollen coracle was never equipped with a carrying strap. 'The customary way of carrying it is to support the seat across the shoulders, steadying the coracle with the hands gripping the sides, close to the fore-end . . . The method of carrying supported by the hands over the head is a comparatively recent innovation. Old photographs show the coracle being carried in the orthodox manner by a leather strap across the breast and shoulders, with the paddle resting horizontally on the left shoulder, with its loom end inserted within the interior of the coracle.'[116] A short 4 foot paddle was used on this type of coracle. The blade 22 inches long was parallel sided, being 4½ inches wide connected to a cylindrical loom without a crutch.

The following are the dimensions of a typical Llangollen two-seater coracle:

Length—57 inches
Beam—Bilge—53 inches
Width of seat—11 inches
Beam—Front—33 inches
Length of seat—39½ inches
Height—front and back—20 inches
Depth to top of seat—14 inches
Height—centre—17 inches
Weight—50lb

The method of construction was described by Hornell as follows:[117]

'After the two sets of laths have been interlaced in the usual manner on a plank flooring, a wooden roller about 3 feet long by about 6 inches in diameter, having an iron pin running through it, is placed lengthwise over the laths on each side, and secured to the floor by iron brackets . . . The two rollers are arranged at a distance apart of about what the eventual gunwale beam is to be. Discarded rollers from an old mangle are suitable for this purpose.

'The projecting parts of the transverse laths, after a preliminary soaking with warm water, are bent up and tacked against the upper part of the rollers on the outer aspect, their ends sloping inwards to form the tumble-home type of side characteristic of this design. After being left for some time to set the bends, the projecting ends, at the proper level, are nailed between a pair of lower gunwale hoops, each composed of two half-hoops, in the Bangor manner, but instead of being arranged horizontally, the half-hoops are fixed with such a sheer towards the ends of the framework that their ends cross one another obliquely amidships. The two rollers are now removed and the seat with its two sets of pillar supports are put in and secured in place; this permits of the nailing on of the upper circumferential hoops to form the gunwale proper. A cover of sailcloth is stretched over the frame; an overlap at each corner strengthens what are the weakest places.'

Conway

James Hornell, when he carried out his survey of coracles in the nineteen-thirties, was of the opinion that coracles were unknown on the Conway and all those in use at the time had 'been imported, two at least from Llechryd on the Teifi'.[118] Hornell was incorrect in his assumption, for coracles were widely used on the river, at least until 1914, and those coracles were quite different from those used on other rivers in north Wales. In 1887, for example, John Jones of Tanrallt, Betws-y-coed, who was licensed to use a basket trap on the Lledr[119] which resulted in litigation in that year, was also licensed to use a coracle for salmon fishing on the Lledr as well as the Conway. His coracle is now at the Welsh Folk Museum, St Fagans.

Undoubtedly coracles were used in large numbers on the Conway, at least from the sixteenth century,[120] and Michael Faraday on his visit to the area in 1819 said: 'Here and there on the river we saw fishermen in their coracles: little vessels something like a washing tub squeezed by a door into an oval form; a board is put across the middle in which two men sit, one each way and whilst one paddles the other casts the net.'[121]

It seems, therefore, that two-man coracles were used on the Conway as they were on parts of the neighbouring Dee. By about 1840 the use of coracles as fishing craft on the Conway had declined very greatly. In evidence to the Commissioners on Salmon Fisheries in 1861[122] a witness said that coracle fishing had ceased in the Llanrwst area, and added that 'below Llanrwst, where the tide comes . . . they were only used where the men could not land their nets; they never used them below Trefriew . . . they fished about seven or eight miles above the tideway and a little lower down for sparlings'. Coracle fishing during the last quarter of the nineteenth century and the first decade of the twentieth seems to have been limited to the Betws-y-coed district, well up river from the tidal reaches.

The Conway coracle.

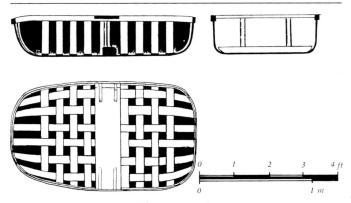

The Conway coracle.

The Conway coracle preserved at the Welsh Folk Museum[123] is unusual in that the framework consists of broad, 3 inch strips of cleft ash interwoven to form a solid-looking frame. The longitudinal laths are 6 in number and these are crossed by 9 other laths. The gunwale is also of ash, each lath being 2 inches wide, and in between the two oval hoops forming the gunwale the ends of the long and cross laths are inserted and nailed in place. On the outside of the gunwale a hoop, similar to that used by coopers for cask making, is nailed to the timber. Above the fifth cross-lath a heavy baulk of timber is nailed and two pillars for supporting the deal seat are inserted in this. The space below the seat does not form a carrying box for fish as in some coracles, but the pillars were used by the fishermen for carrying the coracles on their heads; the pillars acting as hand grips. The Conway, like the Welshpool coracle, is equipped with a carrying strap and the paddle is a long piece of ash without shoulders to the blade and without a hand grip at the top. The blade itself, flat at the front and rounded at the back, is 22 inches long and gradually merges with the round tapering loom of the paddle. The deal seat of the coracle, supported on two wooden pillars, is also strengthened by two pairs of metal straps, nailed to its top and inserted between the two ash laths of the gunwale.

The principal dimensions of the Conway coracle are:

Length—66 inches
Height from ground (seat)—14 inches
Maximum width (at seat)—40 inches
Height from ground (front)—15 inches
Width (front)—38 inches
Height from ground (rear)—13¾ inches
Width (stern)—38 inches
Depth (at seat)—14 inches
Weight—35lb

Severn

A River Board bye-law of 1890 severely restricted and the Salmon and Freshwater Fisheries Act of 1923 spelt the doom of coracle netting on the Severn. Undoubtedly before 1923 more coracles were used on the Severn than any other river in Britain, for coracles were used for a distance of approximately sixty miles along the river between Welshpool in Montgomeryshire and Bewdley in Worcestershire. They persisted until 1939 on a stretch of river extending to about thirty miles between Shrewsbury and Arley, but of course, not officially for salmon netting.[124] Today, a single part-time coracle man, Eustace Rogers, at Ironbridge in Shropshire follows a tradition that is said to have been in his family for over three hundred years.

Unlike the coracles of West Wales, the Severn coracle was never a vessel used specifically for salmon netting and was widely used 'for ferrying, angling, laying lines and the carriage of stone and brick sinkers required for the lines and of the large wicker traps employed in eel fishing'.[125] Since bridges on the Shropshire section of the Severn are few and far between, the coracle was widely used by the inhabitants of Severnside as an easy means of crossing the river. An 'Ironbridge' coracle for this reason is considerably broader and more manoeuvrable than any other type. 'As many as four people were ferried across the river on one occasion by an old man . . . The passengers stood around the paddler clutching his shoulders and each other.'[126] So considerable was the demand for coracles in the Ironbridge district at the beginning of the present century that a school was established where the principles of coracle manipulation were taught.

When coracles were used on the Severn there were three distinct types: 1. The Ironbridge coracle, 2. The Shrewsbury coracle and 3. The Welshpool coracle.

The Ironbridge coracle as made by the late Harry Rogers until his death in the early nineteen-sixties is an almost oval, bowl-shaped craft, approximately 57 inches long and 36 inches wide. The gunwale is almost horizontal, being 14 inches above the ground and the seat is usually 9 inches wide. The coracle weighs no more than 27lb and the framework consists of ten longitudinal and nine cross laths or 'splints', each 1½ inches wide and made of sawn ash. Short lengths of diagonal splints are inserted at the four extremities of the frame to give added strength to the frame, but these four diagonals are only 20 inches long and do not run the length of the frame. The

The Severn coracle: Ironbridge.

gunwale consists of two half-hoops, overlapped and spliced together at the end to form an oval.

Hornell describes the method of constructing the Ironbridge coracle as follows:[127]

'The laths or ''splints'' are bought ready sawn to the proper thickness; they average 8 feet in length. Those for the frames are a fraction under ¼ inch thick, while those for the gunwale hoops are slightly over this thickness. Before use the laths are soaked with hot water to make them supple. When ready, those that are to run fore-and-aft are laid upon a wooden flooring or some sort of wooden platform such as an old door and spaced apart at regular intervals; this done, the transverse laths are interlaced and then, to keep them in place, the laths at the four corners are tacked down to the flooring or platform.

'Prior to this an oval hoop formed of two half-hoops, overlapped and spliced together at the ends, has been prepared of the size and form to be taken by the gunwale. The ends of all the laths, hitherto lying prone on the flooring, are now bent upwards and tacked but not clenched to the outer side of the oval hoop, at a height of about 14 inches from the ground. After this, strings are passed in various directions across the hoop and between the upstanding ends of the bent-up laths, in order to bring them to the proper curvature. These strings prevent the laths from springing out of curve but do not hinder some of them from being pulled inwards, so it becomes necessary to run ''stays'' outwards from their ends to the plank floor to obviate this. These outer stays are particularly required at the corners, which are the most difficult parts of the frame to shape correctly. In this condition and under constant adjustment of the controlling strings, the framework is left for several days for the bends to become set in position. At the end of this time, an outer and permanent hooping—the so-called ''skeleton hoop''—is put on; the first or temporary one being removed thereafter. The projecting ends of the ribs are next cut off level with the top edge of the skeleton hoop. This done, the frame is set free from the tacks holding it to the flooring and turned bottom up in order that the laths may be tarred on their outer side. The framework is also ready to be covered with its ''hide'' of unbleached calico. As bought, this is 1 yard wide, so two widths are overlapped 3 or 4 inches and sewn together.

This seam runs down the centre line of the bottom. When adjusted in position the free margins are turned over the edge of the skeleton hoop and tacked on at short intervals: any excess is trimmed away.

'At this stage the bulkhead, which is to furnish the median support of the seat, is put in. This done, pitch and tar, roughly in the proportion of 1 quart of tar to 2lb of pitch, are boiled together and a coating of the mixture applied over the outside of the cover.

'The following day the two remaining gunwale hoops are added, one on the inner side of the rib ends, the other on the outer side of the skeleton hoop but separated from it by the fabric of the cover. To do this four half-hoops are made by bending laths to the shape required. A cord adjusted between the two ends of each half-hoop keeps them in shape till set. Before, however, fitting the inner hoop, two short strengthening bars are fitted at each corner of the frame, as these places are weak owing to the frame ends diverging here rather widely. The stern half of the inner hoop is put in place first, four iron screw-clamps or ''dogs'' being used to hold it in position while being nailed to the skeleton hoop by 1 inch paris points. In the same way one of the outer stern hoops is put on at the after-end of the frame. Finally the forward half-hoops are put on, one within the frame ends, the other outside the calico cover. Care is taken to allow sufficient overlap at the junction of each set of half-hoops.

'All that remains to be done is to fit the seat in position. This is laid athwart the coracle a little abaft the centre; its ends rest on the gunwale at each side, and each end is secured thereto by three angle ties of iron, 1½ inches long, each screwed in place, the outer ones with one screw through each arm, the middle one with two screws, as these screw into the bulkhead bar, whereas the others screw into the hoops of the gunwale. The seat is further secured by screws or by nails passing through it into the heads of the three bulkhead pillars. Two slots are cut in the seat, each about 8 inches from either end, for the carrying strap of leather, and a thin leather thong-loop is put around the centre seat prop; through this loop the head of the paddle is passed on the foreside when the coracle has to be carried, thereby relieving the pressure upon the chest. As a final touch some owners paint the outer gunwale hoop and the inner faces of the lath frames.'

The paddle used at Ironbridge is almost spadelike in shape, with a broad blade 16 inches long and 7¼ inches wide with a cylindrical loom screwed to it. A straight hand grip 4 inches long at the top runs at right angles to the loom. The whole paddle measures 40 inches long. An older type of paddle in use in the nineteenth century was in one piece. 'The blade', says Hornell, 'is elegantly tapered from the broad distal end upwards to its junction with the loom, which is circular in section. The crutch or grip is a bluntly rounded expansion of the head of the loom. Length 5 feet; blade 30 inches long by 6 inches at the outer end; loom 3½ inches in circumference; crutch 3 inches long. Locally the loom is termed the ''stale'', while the crutch is the ''casp''.'

The following are the principal dimensions of a coracle made by Harry Rogers of Ironbridge in 1955 and now at the Museum of English Rural Life, University of Reading:

Length—57 inches
Height of gunwale—14 inches
Width—43 inches
Width of seat—11 inches

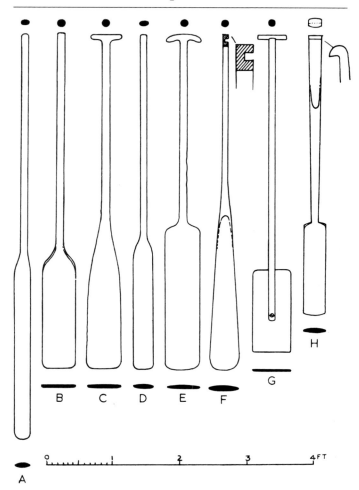

Types of coracle paddle: A Towy; B Wye and Usk; C Severn
(Ironbridge); D Tâf; E Severn (Shrewsbury); F Dee (Bangor);
G Severn (modern Ironbridge); H Teifi

Coracles were in use on the Severn at Shrewsbury until 1939 and they were mainly used at that time by anglers. Hornell points out that some of the coracles he saw in use in the nineteen-thirties had been made on an elaborate wooden mould around which the framework was built. Nevertheless although the mould was used by a Shrewsbury boat builder from about 1880, only six coracles were built on it, and the technique of construction usually adopted by the coracle makers of the town resembled those of Ironbridge.

The Shrewsbury coracle is less oval in shape than the Ironbridge type and like the Wye and Towy coracles it has a distinctly broad bow and a more pointed stern. The framework is noticeably in-curving towards the gunwale, and the front and rear compartments of the coracle are separated by a grating of four uprights crossed at right angles by five ash laths. These laths are of the same width and thickness as those used for the frame and gunwale of the coracle. The gunwale itself consists of three thicknesses of laths nailed together to form a sturdy frame. A half-round hazel hoop is tacked on to the lath gunwale all the way round to give added strength to the framing. Eight lengths of sawn ash splints, each 1½ inches wide and ¼ inches thick, form the longitudinal membranes of the frame. Above them but not interlaced with them are another eight laths at right angles to the longitudinal laths. When the laths cross, a nail is inserted and each lath in turn is nailed between the splints of the gunwale. A pair of diagonals crossing just in front of the seat run the whole length of the coracle, but these again merely rest on the framing and are tacked to them rather than being interlaced. Undoubtedly where sawn ash is used, there would be a danger in cracking the timber if the thin strips of timber were interlaced. The front compartment of the coracle is strengthened with three short cross-pieces tacked to the frame to give added strength at a place where the fisherman would rest his feet.

The Severn coracle: Shrewsbury.

An example of a late nineteenth-century Shrewsbury coracle at the Welsh Folk Museum[128] has the following dimensions:

Length—58 inches
Width (at seat)—33 inches
Depth (at seat)—13¾ inches
Width of seat—8¾ inches
Height of gunwale (back)—10½ inches
Height of gunwale (at seat)—15 inches
Height of gunwale (front)—16 inches
Weight—31lb

In shape and design the coracles of the Welshpool area had close affinities to those of the Wye and Usk. Salmon netting on the upper Severn was prohibited as early as 1890 and coracles were used in the Welshpool area until their final disappearance in the nineteen-thirties for such tasks as retrieving ducks when shooting and for angling. Before 1934 coracles were also used for setting night lines[129] but as a result of legislation at that time setting night lines, like netting salmon, became illegal on the Severn.[130]

Hornell describes the method of constructing a Welshpool coracle as follows:[131]

'The materials required to construct the framework consist of seven ash slats [laths] 7 feet in length and eight others of 5½ feet length; all must be "rent" or cleaved by hand with a hoop shaver to a width of from 1⅛ to 1½ inches by ¼ inches thick; also four more carefully fashioned slats for the gunwale. These obtained, three of the longer ones are laid down upon an old door . . . the outer ones at 2 feet 7 inches apart toward one end and 2 feet 4 inches toward the other. Two short slats are laid transversely across these, 3 feet apart . . . and the points of intersection secured temporarily in position by being tacked through to the door beneath. The remaining four longitudinal slats are next laid down, and then the rest of the cross slats, six in number, are laced in and out of the seven longitudinal ones at about equal distances apart. This gives an open basketry with rectangular meshes about 6 inches along each side.

'Having the four corner points tacked down to the door flooring below, the ends of two of the median longitudinal slats, after softening with hot water, are bent upward and nailed to the outer side of an ovate gunwale frame. A couple of the cross-slats are similarly treated. With these guide frames in position the rest are easily worked into their respective places.

'The inner gunwale band referred to is made up of two lengths of wide ash slats about 1¾ inches wide, each bent into an oval form and joined to its fellow by an overlapped joint. The two oval bands differ markedly in radial curve.

'To stiffen each of the four corners of the frame, a short length of slat is placed diagonally between the gunwale and the second slat crossing from front and side; each is 23 inches long. Other strengthening pieces are four accessory ''foot'' battens, each 3 feet long, placed alternately with the first five transverse frames and nailed over them. When all the framing is in position, the seat is put on. This is a board 8 inches wide, 2 feet 10 inches long at the fore-side and 2 feet 8 inches along the afterside. Each end rests upon the edge of the gunwale band and is screwed to a short batten nailed against its inner face at the place where the ends of the two sections overlap. To hold the bottom stiff, the seat is supported at one-third its length from each end by a stout cylindrical rod about 16 inches in length; its lower end rests upon one of the bottom slats.

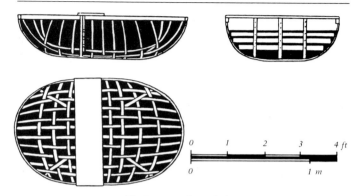

The Severn coracle: Ironbridge.

'At this stage the frame is set free from the holding down nails and is turned bottom up, to have ts cover of stout calico put on. This done, a coat of pitch and tar is applied both to the inner and outer surfaces. Last of all an outer gunwale slat band is nailed to the outer side of the frame ends which are thus enclosed between an outer and an inner gunwale band.'

The ash paddle of the Welshpool coracle has a long narrow blade without distinct shoulders and measure 51 inches long. One side of the blade is flat, the other convex and ther is no hand grip at the top. The Welshpool coracle is not equipped with a carrying strap, and for transporting the vessel 'the coracle is lifted by both hands with the bottom upwards; thus inverted the flat of the seat is brought to rest on the left shoulder; then the paddle is placed across the right shoulder with the blade inserted under the seat in order to take part of the weight. The net, in the days when this was used, was carried on top of the inverted bottom'.[132] It seems that the horizontal method of carrying coracles, without carrying straps being employed, was limited to the upper Severn above Shrewsbury, the Conway and the upper reaches of the Dee. In all other districts, coracles were equipped with carrying straps of leather or withy.

The dimensions of a Welshpool coracle measured by Hornell were as follows: [133]

Overall length—58½ inches
Depth (front)—16 inches
Maximum width—36 inches
Depth (back)—13½ inches

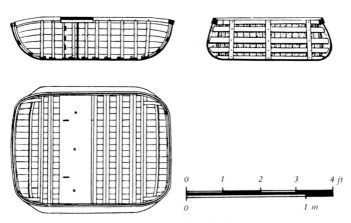

The Severn coracle: Welshpool.

A Leighton Bridge fisherman, who was 78 years of age when recorded in the early thirties by Stanley Davies, described the method of construction as follows:[134]

'This type of coracle has no sheer; if any sheer were given to the fore-end it would be difficult to pull in a salmon out of the net. It is 4 feet 9 inches long, by 3 feet 3 inches wide, and 18 inches deep at the seat. The pointed end is the stern and is called the back. The bow is called the fore-end. The centre of the seat is 2 feet away from the back. The user sits facing the fore-end. The frame is made of ash, riven by hand with a hoop shaver (a cooper's tool). The slats are 1½ inches thick by ¼ inch thick. The interwoven framework is made of 7 slats lengthways and 8 slats broadways, with a short slat added in each corner.

'The coracle is made as follows: An old door is placed on the ground. The slats are laid on and interwoven, and each nailed down in two places to the door. Only slats which have been riven can be interwoven. If the more modern method of using sawn laths is adopted the laths must be nailed together with copper nails. The ends of the slats are then softened with hot water, and bent up to meet the inside rim of the gunwale. The slats are then nailed to the gunwale. The nails should be flat-headed clog nails, as they are soft enough to be clinched, but they are difficult to obtain. The gunwale is of ash, and is 13 feet 4 inches long. Owing to the difficulty of obtaining such a long length it can be in two pieces which meet under the seat. In addition four slats are laid on the bottom of the coracle to take the pressure of the user's feet. There are also two round pieces of timber one inch in diameter one end of which is screwed to the underside of the seat and the other end to the bottom of the coracle to distribute the weight of the seat. The frame is then covered with calico and waterproofed inside and out with a mixture of 2lb pitch and 1lb of tar. The outer rim of the gunwale is then nailed on. Two short strips are nailed to the gunwale to help to support the seat. The seat is 8 inches wide and is fixed last of all. Alongside the left hand side of the seat is kept the ''priest'', a stout oak stick about a foot long used for

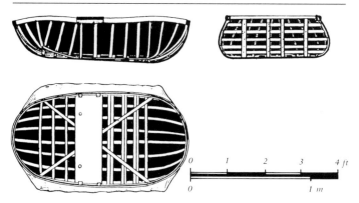

The Severn coracle: Lower Severn—Shrewsbury.

stunning the salmon. It is hung just below the gunwale in two loops of leather.

'The paddle 4 feet 3 inches long, has the edges of one side of the blade champhered, and this side must be kept "next to the water", which you are drawing towards you; otherwise you will find yourself out of the coracle and in the water. There are two ways of using the paddle. One is to pull the coracle through the water by placing the paddle in the water in front of you, and, using both hands, working the paddle in a figure eight, keeping the champhered side of the blade towards you, "next to the water" which you are drawing towards you. When netting you place the paddle in the water on the right hand side of the coracle, and tuck your arm round it, with the top of the shaft resting on your forearm, and your fingers over and equally divided each side of the shaft. The left hand is then free to handle the net line.

'I prefer to carry the coracle horizontally and inverted, lifting it up and letting the flat of the seat rest on the left shoulder;

then I place the paddle on my right shoulder, and let the blade fit under the seat to take part of the weight. The net is thrown over the top [really the inverted bottom] of the coracle, which avoids the user getting wet from the net. If you carry the coracle on your back by means of a strap looped to the seat, the wind is liable to fill the coracle and blow you off your feet.

'Materials used to construct a Severn Coracle.

Ash:

7 Lengthway slats, 7 feet 0 inches

8 Broadway slats, 5 feet 0 inches

4 Corner pieces, 2 feet 0 inches (all 1¼ inches x ¼ inch)

4 Pieces under feet, 2 feet 0 inches

4 Pieces for gunwale, 7 feet 0 inches x 1¼ inches x ¼ inch

2 Seat struts, 1 foot 6 inches x 1¼ inches

Deal:

Seat, 3 feet 6 inches x 8 inches x¾ inch, planed, self edge

2 Seat supports, 8 inches x 1½ inches x ¾ inch

Oak:

''Priest'', 12 inches x 2 inches diameter

Ash Paddle:

4 feet 3 inches x 4½ inches x 1 inch

'To complete the coracle the following materials are required—calico, pitch, tar, leather loops, copper nails, iron clog nails.

'In transit a hole can be stopped by a clay clod, taken from the river bank and held in place with the foot. Large holes were repaired with patches of calico painted over with hot pitch. Small holes were repaired with hot pitch, but now it is more convenient to warm a stick of gutta-percha with a match and apply it to the hole. Constant painting and repairing steadily increases the weight of the coracle.'

Although the use of the coracle as a fishing craft in the present century has been limited to the above rivers, in the nineteenth century their use was far more widespread. In south Wales, for example, bowl-shaped nearly square coracles were used on the River Loughor at Pontardulais, a stream that became heavily polluted during the last quarter of the century.

The Loughor was a particularly good salmon and sewin river in the late eighteenth and early nineteenth century, says Donovan[135] in describing Swansea market. 'Half a dozen females seated upon the panniers of their ponies . . . rode hastily down the market place with a supply of sewen . . . conveyed from Pontardulais, about ten miles to the westward . . . abounding with fish during the summer, being caught in the coracle fisheries by peasantry.'

The Dyfi in mid-Wales, another river that became heavily polluted with effluence from lead mines, was also a coracle-fishing river. In 1800 Bingley described coracles that were from '5 feet to 6 feet long and 3 feet and 4 feet broad, of an oval shape, so light that one man may with ease carry them on his shoulder'.[136] By 1861 coracle netting, due to pollution and the influence of the Dovey Fishery Association, had ceased and the 24 coracles operating on the river were declared illegal, although a few years previously 'there was an immense deal of coracle fishing'.[137]

FOOTNOTES

93. At the Welsh Folk Museum, St Fagans, the following types of coracle have been preserved. Towy, Tâf, Teifi, Upper Dee, Lower Dee, Conway, Severn (upper), Wye. A Severn coracle (Ironbridge type) has been preserved at the City of Gloucester Museum and a Wye coracle at the Hereford Museum.

94. *Minutes of Evidence, op, cit*, p 130.

95. Hornell, *op, cit*, p 41.

96. Miss M L Wight of Hereford photographed a number of Cleddadu coracles in the nineteen-thirties. Her negatives are now in the collections of the Welsh Folk Museum and provide an irreplacable record of coracle fishing in west Wales.

97. *Camden's Brittania* translated by E Gibson. Column 590 [London 1695].

98. Twiston-Davies, L and Averyl Edwards: *Welsh Life in the Eighteenth Century* (London 1939), p 53.

99. Clark, J H: *Usk—Past and Present* (Usk no date), pp 161—2.

100. Public Notice Usk and Ebbw Fishery District 1866. Deposited at Brecknock Museum.

101. A coracle at the Hereford City Museum was used on the Wye for fishing by Mr William Dew of Ross-on-Wye, until 1910. It is believed that this was the last coracle in use in the Ross district. They did persist for a little longer in the Monmouth and Redbrook districts.

102. Cox, E: *Historical Tour through Monmouthshire* (Brecon 1804), 282.

103. Anonymous: *Travels in Great Britain* (London 1805), 2, pp 39—40.

104. *Minutes of Evidence, op, cit* , pp 30, 33, 34.

105. Gilbert, H A: *The Tale of a Wye Fisherman* (London 1929), p 36.

106. Hornell, *op, cit*, p 264.

107. On loan to the Welsh Folk Museum 1972.

108. Hornell, *op, cit*, pp 265—6.

109. Hughes-Parry, J: *A Salmon Fisherman's Notebook* (London 1862), p 22.

110. *Minutes of Evidence,op, cit*, p 224.

111. *First Annual Report of the Inspectors of Salmon Fishries* (London, 2nd ed 1955), p 18.

112. *Second Annual Report of the Inspectors of Salmon Fisheries* (London 1863), p 13.

113. *First Annual Report, op, cit*, p 22.

114. Hughes-Parry, *op, cit*, p 19.

115. Hornell, *op, cit*, p 228.

116. *Ibid*, p 292.

117. *Ibid*, p 292.

118. *Ibid*, p 287.

119. See Chapter 5.

120. National Library of Wales MS. 8589 B.

121. Tomos, Dafydd: *Michael Faraday in Wales* (Denbigh 1972), p 95.

122. *Minutes of Evidence, op, cit*, p 205.

123. Accession Number 69.262.

124. Hornell, *op, cit*, p 272.

125. Coracles were also used on the Worcestershire Avon in the eighteenth century.

126. Hornell, *op, cit*, p 273.

127. *Ibid*, pp 274—5.

128. Accession Number 37.290/1.

129. Hornell, *op, cit*, p 277, states 'There are two ways of setting night lines. One is to use a number of lines, each about 15 yards long and fastened to a stake in the bank. The other is to use a line about 200 yards long and to set it from a coracle zig-zag in the bed of the river'.

130. Davies, A S: 'The River Trade and Craft of Montgomeryshire', *Mont. Coll.*, Vol 44, (1938—6), p 47.

131. *Ibid*, pp 178—9.

132. Hornell, *op, cit*, p 288.

133. Unfortunately no example of a Welshpool coracle has been preserved.

134. Davies, *op, cit, (Mont. Coll.)*, pp 47—8.

135. Donovan, *op, cit*, 2QR, p 148.

136. Bingley, W: *A Tour Round North Wales* (1800), Vol 1, p 470.

137. *Minutes of Evidence, op, cit*, (1861), p 176.